"Craig is the real deal, seeking to s   r
expatriates participating in God's mission. When the spotlight falls
on him, as it does with his writing and speaking, he redirects it to
others, to the insider guardians of the gospel who are teaching us the
ways of indigenous missions. The greatest challenge in missions
today is for people of privilege to remove ourselves from the center.
Anyone who is an outsider to the people they're ministering with is
privileged, otherwise we could not afford to be there. In this book, re-
imagining the ascension gifts for crosscultural application, Craig
draws on his hard-learned experience to challenge outsiders to
become 'alongsiders.' Truly understood, the prophetic call carried
along by Craig's pithy turns of phrase should bring us to our knees,
surrendering our condescensions in penitent humility."

Jay Matenga, director of the Global Witness Department,
World Evangelical Alliance

"This book overflows with Christ-centered, culturally sensitive
wisdom gained from the practical experience of serving the poor in
rural Cambodia. It challenged me repeatedly to reevaluate why and
how outsiders like me should respond to God's calling to serve local
communities. Craig Greenfield offers a unique insider's perspective
on how he and the 'alongsiders' humbly applied the missional calling
of Ephesians 4 in ways that honored the local context. His well-
structured guidance is easy to read, compelling, and inspiring to
follow. Reading this is to stand on the shoulders of giants who dare
to be catalysts, allies, seekers, midwives, and guides rather than
saviors and CEOs."

Christo Greyling, senior director for faith and external engagement
at World Vision International

"Personality and spiritual inventories are often trendy but not
always biblically grounded. This book has the feel of a spiritual inventory but is utterly based in Scripture. It also has concomitant
pitfalls to avoid, plus the author's rich crosscultural experience to
inform it, uniquely translating into practical ways to serve in
overseas contexts. This is a combination nicely balanced and definitely needed for today's globalized world as we endeavor to embody
Jesus' upside-down kingdom."

Allen Yeh, professor of intercultural studies and missiology
at Biola University

"Books on the Ephesians 4 typology of ministry (APEST) are rare enough. Rarer still are those that seek to translate these critical biblical forms into the language of crosscultural mission. Craig's is a practical and wise book that does precisely that. We are grateful."

Alan Hirsch, founder of the 5Q Collective and author of *5Q: Reactivating the Original Intelligence and Capacity of the Body of Christ*

"For too long the power and economic disparities of Western missionaries have obscured or undermined their contributions in marginalized communities. Finally, here is a book that provides a helpful framework to guide the gifted outsider and grant dignity to the knowledgeable insider. People from distant contexts and those who've lived their whole lives in difficult neighborhoods—we need each other to solve some of the most pernicious ministry challenges. *Subversive Mission* will clarify for the reader how locals and foreigners can work together for lasting, healthy change."

Scott Bessenecker, director of global engagement and justice for InterVarsity Christian Fellowship/USA

"A bold, illuminating, and timely book. Essential reading for every person who wants to be a danger *for* the kingdom and not *to* the kingdom."

Ken Shigematsu, pastor of Tenth Church, Vancouver, and author of *Survival Guide for the Soul*

"Over the past few years, the church has been rediscovering a fresh vision of the fivefold gifts presented in Ephesians 4. Many are recognizing, often for the first time, the significance of all five of the 'APEST' gifts. In *Subversive Mission*, Craig Greenfield helps to propel this important conversation forward by assisting the reader in seeing the fivefold not simply as ministry types but as missional types, especially in a crosscultural setting where we need to empower indigenous leaders. If you want to understand how the church can better engage God's kingdom activity around the world, read this book."

Brad Brisco, author of *Missional Essentials* and *Covocational Church Planting*

SUBVERSIVE MISSION

SERVING AS OUTSIDERS

IN A WORLD OF NEED

CRAIG GREENFIELD

An imprint of InterVarsity Press
Downers Grove, Illinois

InterVarsity Press
P.O. Box 1400 | Downers Grove, IL 60515-1426
ivpress.com | email@ivpress.com

InterVarsity Press® is the publishing division of InterVarsity Christian Fellowship/USA®.
For more information, visit intervarsity.org.

All Scripture quotations, unless otherwise indicated, are taken from The Holy Bible, New International Version®,
NIV®. Copyright © 1973, 1978, 1984, 2011 by Biblica, Inc.™ Used by permission of Zondervan. All rights
reserved worldwide. www.zondervan.com. The "NIV" and "New International Version" are trademarks
registered in the United States Patent and Trademark Office by Biblica, Inc.™

Published in association with Gardner Literary, LLC. www.gardner-literary.com.

While any stories in this book are true, some names and identifying information may have been changed to
protect the privacy of individuals.

The publisher cannot verify the accuracy or functionality of website URLs used in this book beyond the date of
publication.

Cover design and image composite: David Fassett
Interior design: Jeanna Wiggins

ISBN 978-1-5140-0438-8 (print) | ISBN 978-1-5140-0480-7 (digital)

Printed in the United States of America ⊛

Library of Congress Cataloging-in-Publication Data
A catalog record for this book is available from the Library of Congress.

29 28 27 26 25 24 23 22 | 9 8 7 6 5 4 3 2 1

For my parents, Dave and Dawn Greenfield,

who went before,

and showed me the way.

CONTENTS

▲ ▼ ▲

This is a work of creative nonfiction. Though it is a true story, I have relied on my own memory, unpublished writings, and past blog posts of events and conversations. Many of those conversations are translated from their original language into English. I have also compressed and reordered the timeline where necessary and simplified the narrative arc in a way that I hope will make sense to the reader.

All profits from this book will support vulnerable children in Cambodia, allowing them to attend camps at Shalom Valley. By purchasing this book, you are contributing to the joy and laughter that arises in that magical moment when a child sees the ocean for the first time.

INTRODUCTION

It takes a spider to repair its own web.

ANCIENT KHMER PROVERB

MY PHONE LIGHTS UP AND PINGS WITH A MESSAGE. I flick my thumb across the screen and an invitation appears. The backlighting on my phone illuminates my face as I read the invitation of a lifetime.

"Brother Craig," it begins, as so many messages from my friends in India do. Relationships are everything in this part of the world. "Would you come and speak at our upcoming Christian event in Delhi? You would be our keynote speaker. There will be twenty thousand young leaders in attendance. We want you to challenge them to reach out and walk alongside children in their communities. You can really get your Alongsiders message out, Brother!"

Twenty thousand young leaders! My eyebrows lift, and a whistle of amazement escapes my lips. For some, public speaking is their worst nightmare. Speaking to twenty thousand young leaders would be daunting for most people—and frankly, it's daunting for me too. But I have been sharing about God's heart for the poor at conferences, festivals, and churches for years, and an opportunity to spread the vision like this is an amazing dream for me, a chance to use my God-given talents to grow the Alongsiders ministry and reach thousands of children.

I start thinking through logistics and imagining the potential impact. And if I'm honest, I begin to imagine myself on that stage, the audience in rapt attention. Some good photos of the crowds for my social media feed wouldn't hurt at all. I'm only human.

I press my forefinger on the message until it turns a darker shade, then hit the forward button. Before responding, I know that I need to submit the invitation to my mentor and South Indian friend, Paulus.

My connection with India goes back to my paternal grandparents, who were missionaries in South India for twenty-five years. My father spent his early years in Bangalore. My parents were also missionaries, so I guess you might say that being an outsider working for change in the world runs in my blood.

Paulus has been helping me navigate these types of situations in India for years, and as an outsider, I'm careful to listen to his insider advice. But as I wait for Paulus's response, my heart begins to sink a little as I anticipate what he will say. I know Paulus well.

His message eventually pops up on my phone. "Brother! Call me when you can." Relationships are everything in India.

I press video dial with trepidation, and within seconds, I am greeted by Paulus's smiling face and rich, baritone voice. A

Tamil by ethnicity, he has a very dark complexion, and he is wearing his thick, trademark black glasses. They frame the kindest eyes, which shine with spiritual wisdom and friendship.

I want to make sure he understands what this invitation means to me, so I almost start to say, "This is the invitation of a lifetime, Paulus!" But I hold my tongue and wait for my mentor to speak.

"Ah yes," he smiles. "I don't think this is a good opportunity for us, ahhha? This will put a big spotlight on you as a foreigner. If we want this discipleship movement to take off here as a local Indian movement, it would be better for it not to be presented by you. That will send the wrong impression, Craig."

His words are understated but crystal clear. They immediately remind me of the ancient Khmer proverb, "It takes a spider to repair its own web." My chest sinks, and I feel my lips curve into a slight frown. I know Paulus is right, but, frankly, I'm gutted. After I hang up, I sit for a while, letting the disappointment sink in.

Now, at this point in the story you may be thinking, *Needs are needs. Who cares who meets them? Get out there and make a difference! Seize every opportunity to use your God-given gifts to preach the gospel!*

But what if the greater invitation for many of us in this new era—particularly those of us who have power and privilege—is to use more wisdom in the ways we seek to serve others? I've had to learn this lesson the hard way as I have lived for two decades in slums and inner cities and made a lot of mistakes along the way. Though I've started ministries around the world, I am still learning.

As a white Westerner, I have always been taught to consider the words I speak on stage as if they stand alone—disembodied—as if I am a neutral messenger bringing the word of God. After all, it's not like I would be up there on stage waving a Union Jack—the flag of India's former colonial power (and the birthplace of my ancestors). And it's not like I would be flashing wads of cash, implying that by joining this discipleship movement these poor youth could get connected to overseas money.

But I don't need those props to send the youth a message about power and outside money. My very presence sends that message all by itself. Though twenty thousand young leaders would hear my words of love and goodwill, those words would be reinterpreted and misunderstood if I were the person delivering them. I knew in my gut that Paulus was right. The leaders would perceive my words as a foreign message, wrapped in a cloak of colonialism and cash.

The next day, I shoot Paulus a message. "You're absolutely right, Bro. Who else could we get on that stage to communicate the message? Someone local, of course!"

Paulus replies immediately, "I know just the person."

THE TEMPTATION TO PURSUE
GOOD IN THE WRONG WAY

Have you ever noticed how the things that Satan tempted Jesus with during his forty days in the desert were not inherently evil (Lk 4:1-15)? Satan tried to goad Jesus into making bread from stones, but there's nothing particularly bad about bread, is

4

there? Starving people need food, and the world is full of pressing needs. Only a heartless jerk would deny a starving beggar a yummy bread roll.

What about the promise of safety in the hands of angels? That's not evil either! Endangered people need protection. Vulnerable children need people to stand on their side when life is tough. They need someone to get up on a stage somewhere and advocate for their well-being.

And what about the opportunity to have the whole world bow before Jesus? That's not evil either. Imagine if people all over the world knew the love of God. Surely anyone pursuing that end, in any manner, is simply doing the work of God?

And yet, we know from this story that it was the bad guy—Satan himself—dangling all these good things, these valid and pressing needs, in front of Jesus. Still Jesus resisted. He resisted the shortcuts because he knew there was a better way: God's way, God's timing. He resisted the shortcuts because the end never, ever justifies the means.

Jesus could have overwhelmed Israel with his power and wonders—a one-man miracle machine. Instead, he chose the slow, difficult route of raising up a community of believers and empowering them to take his message to the world. He sparked a grassroots movement that has stood the test of time.

What if the temptation we face as people with power and privilege in a world of need is not so much the temptation to pursue evil—rape, murder, or pillaging? Instead, what if our temptation is to pursue good in the wrong way? This is a temptation I face every day because, as a Western missionary for more than twenty years, I walk the streets with forms of power that many of my Cambodian neighbors don't have. I receive invitations and open doors that others don't receive. With that access comes the temptation to be their "savior," to use my power to create "miracles," when I'm really called to be something else—something more humble, vulnerable, and much, much better.

This challenge is for all those who serve as outsiders. It's for anyone who goes into the world seeking to change it while carrying more power than those whom you are trying to reach—whether through a passport or privilege, money or mastery. The simple fact that you have the ability to buy and read a book written in English means you have forms of privilege and power that most people in the world don't have. And that means this book is for you.

I've lived in slums and inner cities among the poor and marginalized for twenty years. I've led humanitarian organizations, a global missions agency, and now a grassroots youth movement that is truly making the world a more beautiful place. I have held the dying and walked alongside the desperate. My whole life is geared toward seeking change that will make the world a better place for everyone.

And, frankly, I'm impatient! I want a better world for my poor neighbors—and I want it sooner rather than later. I want to see more vulnerable children being reached and uplifted. I want bread for the hungry, I want safety for the endangered, and I long for people to know the boundless love of Jesus.

Yet, I've come to understand that there are lots of ways to seek what is good for the world. Over time, I've learned that many of the short-term ways I've tried to pursue change—such as handing out money or food—have actually resulted in more deeply entrenched systems and structures, which continue to perpetuate poverty and injustice. At times, some of my "great ideas" have actually made things much, much worse because I've been trying to play God in the lives of the poor.

So, if we're no longer standing center stage as outsiders, giving keynotes to twenty thousand young leaders, how is God calling us to serve in this new era? Didn't Jesus call us to go out into all the world to make disciples and build his upside-down kingdom? Didn't God call us to bring good news to the poor, freedom for those in captivity, and comfort to those who mourn?

In Ephesians 4:11-13, Paul describes five different types of giftedness for serving God in the world and the church: apostles, prophets, evangelists, shepherds (pastors), and teachers. I believe that these five types continue to provide a promising framework for how we can serve the world even in our postcolonial era, but we need to examine them through different eyes. We can't simply transplant them into crosscultural situations that have deeply embedded power dynamics, or we run the risk of disempowering local people.

For example, perhaps you are a gifted pastor or church planter in Portland. Does this mean you should be a pastor or church planter in Bangalore, India? After all, you will eventually return home, and your foreign ways will be hard to replicate by local people with fewer resources. Perhaps a more effective role would be to come alongside local Indian Christians as a midwife, supporting them as they lead and give birth to what God has already planted in their hearts. During the journey to India, the gifted pastor needs to become a midwife.

Or you may be an apostolically gifted entrepreneur in San Francisco. Does this mean you should initiate new projects among African Americans in inner-city Detroit? Perhaps a wiser approach would be to serve as a catalyst, helping local leaders create new initiatives that reflect their own understanding of their local needs so they will have ownership of them going forward. Sometime during the journey to Detroit, the gifted apostle needs to become a catalyst.

Or perhaps you are a prophetic social justice activist in Toronto. Does this qualify you to lead justice work in Nairobi, Kenya? Perhaps a more helpful role would be to come alongside local activists as an ally, amplifying the voices of those who will continue to live in the local context after the struggle. After all, you can leave at any time, escaping the consequences that local people face after a confrontation. Sometime during the journey to Kenya, the gifted prophet needs to be transformed into an ally.

Each of the five ministry gifts outlined in Ephesians 4—apostle, prophet, evangelist, pastor, and teacher—needs to be reframed for crosscultural contexts, especially in places of poverty, or where there is a significant power differential. The fivefold *ministry* types become *missional* types. Otherwise, we run the risk of playing benevolent gods—taking power away from those who need to be inspired to look to Jesus, the one true Savior. In every context, we need to ask ourselves whether we are ministering as an *insider* or an *outsider.*

In the urban hubs of Asia, the slums of Haiti, the inner cities of North America, and the rural villages of Mexico, those of us who come as outsiders with access to resources tend to hold dramatically more power and money. We often wield that power in heavy-handed ways, knocking over the carefully arranged banquet set before us by our local friends. This lack of self-awareness leads to the sins of colonialism and the "white savior" label, no matter what color you are.

By rethinking these five roles from Ephesians with a cross-cultural perspective, we retain the original meanings, which were meant for insiders, but in ways that don't leave us, as outsiders, hogging the limelight. In place of the traditional translation for Paul's ministry roles in Ephesians, I propose the following five missional types for outsiders in a crosscultural context: *catalyst* (for apostle), *ally* (for prophet), *seeker* (for evangelist), *midwife* (for pastor), and *guide* (for teacher).

As we broaden our thinking about how we might go into the world, we also need to be wise about the minefields that we'll be crossing so we can avoid making the same missteps as those who have gone before us. Not doing so would be a tragic irony. When it comes to vulnerable people's lives, our good intentions do not matter as much as the eventual outcomes.

Rethinking these roles in our own contexts will require some serious self-reflection. Following each chapter outlining one of these five new ways of engaging with the world as outsiders, I'll provide a chapter identifying one of the five major dangers that we urgently need to address: power, complicity, secularism, money, and individualism. Each of these corresponds loosely to one of the fivefold missional types, though we can all fall prey to any of these dangers because they come with the territory of ministering as outsiders. The following is a description of each of the five missional types.

Catalyst (Outsider) / Apostle (Insider). Catalysts are wired as pioneers for the kingdom, not just the church. In their commitment to God's people around the world, they are self-disciplined and mature enough to say, not "my kingdom" but "your kingdom come, Lord." Catalysts refuse to build their own empires but seek to help spark something new in partnership with those insider apostles who will lead the movement going forward. By nature, they are future oriented and want to work with local people in new and uncharted contexts.

Ally (Outsider) / Prophet (Insider). Allies know God's heart for the marginalized, so they seek to come alongside and use their privilege to amplify voices that are struggling to be heard. They care deeply about justice and mercy and are bold enough to speak truth to power in situations of injustice. As outsiders, they are uniquely positioned to question the status quo and call the global community toward God's kingdom on earth, using their privilege (access, training, and resources) to support the causes championed by local prophets.

Seeker (Outsider) / Evangelist (Insider). Seekers search for cultural touchpoints as a way of bridging the universal truth of the gospel with local understanding. They are enthusiasts for contextualization, storytelling, and creativity. As outsiders, they arrive as students of language and culture and are more likely to ask questions than to offer answers. They work with insider evangelists to understand and communicate what the kingdom of God looks like in each new context.

Midwife (Outsider) / Pastor (Insider). Midwives are pastorally gifted leaders who nurture and protect the people of God, helping insider pastors birth, shepherd, and care for communities of faith. As outsiders, they are passionate about cultivating the local church and developing disciples without needing to be in the limelight. They are careful to use church-planting approaches that can be replicated without outside resources.

Guide (Outsider) / Teacher (Insider). Guides are gifted teachers who can not only understand and explain truth but can guide local people to discover the truth for themselves. Guides communicate God's wisdom in all kinds of ways as they help local people discern God's will. Rather than offering prepackaged answers, guides creatively help people work together to discover solutions for themselves.

CHALLENGE TO SERVE AS AN OUTSIDER

Each of us will find ourselves inhabiting different missional types at different times and in different situations, so don't skip to the chapter you think most applies to you. If you do that, the unfolding story won't make sense, and you'll miss valuable information. Instead, engage with each posture as I've had to do, working outside my comfort zone in places of great need.

This book is the story of my own experiments—and failures— as I have tried to grapple with my place in the world and embrace the gifts God has given me. Too often, I have come in as an outsider and taken over from insiders. Too often, I have blundered ahead and trampled on people's toes. Too often, I have failed to empower those on the inside of a local culture. I hope you can learn from my mistakes as the story unfolds.

This book is for every person who has a passionate longing to see God's love change the world but a distaste for the negative baggage of traditional colonial missions. It is for every globally minded follower of Jesus who recognizes that the world doesn't need more "white saviors"—or saviors of any color—but it also doesn't need more apathetic or disengaged Christians. It is for those who know that our guilt and tears, our "thoughts and prayers," mean nothing to the poor and marginalized in the Majority World, unless they are matched with action.

As followers of Jesus, we are all called to be ready to follow Jesus to the ends of the earth right where we are—from Vancouver to Nairobi, from Chicago to Phnom Penh. This is an invitation for each of us to wake up and start acknowledging our weaknesses and humbly composting our crap so that it can enrich the earth wherever we are.

The world needs each of us, but we can't afford to isolate ourselves any longer. Before we head out to change the world, we must first be honest about the power we're carrying. As I share my journey, with all its flaws and mess-ups, I hope you will join me in seeking a better way, a more beautiful vision for how we can all bear the light we have been given into the world.

1

CALLED AND CONFUSED

If you want to change the world,
you have to change the metaphor.

JOSEPH CAMPBELL

AFTER LIVING IN THE SLUMS of Phnom Penh for seven years, my wife, Nay, and I had become disillusioned by many of the ineffective missionary efforts we saw in Asia, so we decided to try something new. We wanted to practice "reverse mission," taking the things we had learned about radical hospitality from our Cambodian neighbors and bringing them to the West.

Our family relocated to Vancouver, Canada, with a dream to extend the welcome of Jesus to those who were not always welcome in Canadian society. "Cook too much food, invite too many people," became our dinner mantra, and we invited the people who didn't fit in anywhere else—the lost and the overlooked, the homeless and the addicted, those who struggled to measure up or toe the line, those living in the shadows of the world's "most livable city." Some nights we had as many as thirty or forty people crowded into our house to share a home-cooked, family-style meal and get some respite from the streets.[1]

When my friend Kevin showed up one night for a meal and a game of pool, he proudly announced that he wanted to become a missionary in Cambodia.

"Two weeks ago you were hunched over a crack pipe on the corner of Main and Hastings, and now you're telling me you want to be a missionary?" I asked as I leaned across the pool table and used the triangle to scoop the balls into position for the break.

"I want to give back, do something good in the world," Kevin told me. "God showed me a picture of me digging ditches in Cambodia." Kevin handed me the pool cue so I could take the first shot.

Kevin had recently quit a crack cocaine addiction after hitting rock bottom in a dingy, Downtown Eastside Vancouver hotel room just down the road from our house.[2] After years in construction, Kevin was now dreaming of using his handyman skills to help the poor in Cambodia. Looking at Kevin's blond hair and pasty white skin, I didn't ask if he had considered that Cambodian handymen might be more suited to the task of digging ditches in the searing Cambodian heat.

Frankly, I was cynical. And, practically speaking, I knew that very few people from Kevin's background could jump through all the hoops to join a missions agency: fund raising, psychological tests, seminary studies. The missions industrial complex is large, expensive, and exclusive.

Then Kevin asked if he could keep coming by for dinner and missionary training.

"Well, everyone is welcome here," I grinned. "But keep in mind, the first time you come, you're our guest. The second time you come, you're a part of the family—and that means helping with the dishes and anything else that needs doing."

Over the next few months, Kevin became a regular fixture in the house, sharing meals and helping us wash up. Eventually, he moved in and began helping with our drug outreach in the neighborhood.

By the time Kevin had been living with us for a year and a half, we could see his rare ability to reach out to folks struggling with addictions in a cut-through-the-crap way that flowed directly from his own experiences. People on the streets called him "the Weeping Preacher" because he got choked up every time he started sharing his story of freedom. He was a key leader in our little Vancouver community, and while I felt that Kevin could do a lot more good in the Downtown Eastside of Vancouver, where he was an insider, Kevin continued to feel that God was calling him to move to Cambodia and serve as an outsider. Though I remained dubious, Kevin persisted, and several months later, I found myself hugging him goodbye outside Vancouver's international departure terminal.

THE WAKE-UP CALL

Shortly after Kevin's departure, I was seated in my doctor's office, waiting to hear the results of some tests I'd had after a particularly bad bout of bleeding. I'd been half sick most of my adult life, an ongoing illness I had written off as "parasites" from years of drinking dirty water in Cambodian slums.

I usually tried to ignore it, but the symptoms had been getting worse, and I'd been working with a specialist to find the right treatment.

The doctor shuffled the papers on his desk, then looked up at me with a concerned sigh. "I'm afraid the results aren't good," he said. "You have colon cancer. We're going to have to operate immediately."

My mind began to spin, and I gripped the arms of the chair, trying to retain control. As my mind threatened to slip into chaos, I pretended to listen to his instructions, then stumbled from the room in a daze.

I don't really remember the bus ride home, but I got back right at dinner time. As usual, the house was full of a boisterous assortment of neighborhood characters, homeless friends laughing it up and messing around. But I just couldn't face anybody that night; I kissed Nay and whispered that I was going to take an early night. I crept up to my room and lay on my bed in the darkness.

After years of serving the fatherless in Cambodia and welcoming those without a family in Canada, there was a good chance that my own two children might now be left without a dad. I had dedicated my life to serving vulnerable children. Now my own would be at risk. "How could this be fair?" I asked God. "How is this your will? What will my future hold?"

Over the coming months, these questions occupied my thoughts and haunted my prayer life. I was in and out of the hospital, and recovery took much longer than I expected, but one question began to dominate my thinking: If you only had five more years to walk this earth, how would you spend those years?

Five years was not so short a time that I would simply spend my final days saying goodbye to family. And not so long that I would lose any sense of urgency. Thinking about those five years helped me focus my thoughts on something meaningful. What would I do with five more years if I were lucky enough to have them?

As I lay in that hospital bed, barely able to move, barely able to get up, every day seemed more precious, every moment more significant. I realized that all the other questions that had been buzzing around in my head were complaints and uncertainties that I was addressing to God, but this question was one that God was asking me. Even as my body was failing, my vision began to focus, and I knew how I would answer this critical question. If I only had five more years to walk this earth, I'd want to spend them doing what God had already called me to do: working for the well-being of the world's most vulnerable children.

As I held this revelation, I sensed that God was inviting me to leave Canada and become an outsider in a crosscultural context again. But the world had shifted since we'd moved to Vancouver, which made this revelation seriously troubling. Public opinion had tilted firmly against outsider efforts to bring change in foreign countries.

Take the cases of two famous missionaries: Jim Elliot and John Allen Chau. In 1956, Jim Elliot was killed by a spear while attempting to make contact with the Huaorani tribe in Ecuador.

He was immediately hailed as a hero and a missionary martyr on the cover of *Life* magazine.[3] His death galvanized and inspired Christians around the world.

Just over sixty years later, in 2017, John Allen Chau was also killed by a spear as he attempted to make contact with the Sentinelese in the Andaman Islands off the coast of India. But this time the worldwide press almost universally labeled him as a fool and a flag-bearer for colonialism. The *New York Times* quoted critics, who called Chau "uninformed, arrogant and self-serving." His death divided Christians around the world. Even *Christianity Today* grappled with Chau's death, lamenting, "For many, missions is a story of heroes and gospel advance. For others, missions is a story of colonialism, genocide, triumphalism, and cross-cultural disasters."[4]

After years of living in Cambodian slums and watching outsiders parachute in, I too had grown discouraged about the role of missionaries in bringing change. Some foreigners arrived, their pockets bulging with money, to set up unsustainable projects in a circus of good intentions. Some planted flashy Western-style churches that couldn't be maintained or replicated by local people without fundraising campaigns, and their bumbling presentations of the gospel were often tainted by foreign culture and values.

In my analysis, there were too many white saviors and not enough wise servants—too many wannabe superheroes and not enough willing sidekicks. It seemed that the whole system was built on a house of expensive cards. The missionary efforts I had observed required raising a ton of financial support, which excluded people from less-resourced communities, such as my friend Kevin. There were also lengthy missionary training requirements, and while this process is good, it tends to exclude those who don't have the resources to take the time out for study.

I wasn't surprised that a growing number of Christians and even church leaders were discarding the traditional model of missions. Many were asking, Why shackle ourselves to an over-engineered system that creates so much animosity, excludes so many people, and closes so many doors? I knew I didn't want to participate in such an enterprise, but I wondered if there might be a different path.

FIGHT, FLIGHT, OR FREEZE?

During my early years living in the slums of Cambodia's capital, Phnom Penh, I came face to face with the fact that I often slipped into the role of a white savior.

A false savior, of any race, plays the role of a benevolent god in the lives of vulnerable people. Of course, our poor neighbors were often grateful for the concrete help we provided. At least it was better than languishing under the jackboot of the malevolent gods in their lives—local loan sharks, traffickers, and corrupt politicians. But those playing the role of god do not transform people's place in the world. The vulnerable people remain dependent on the rich and powerful, both the benevolent and the malevolent. Yet God's beautiful plan is for people to look to *him* so they can become agents of their *own* transformation.

In my high school biology class, I had learned that the natural reaction to any challenge tends to be fight, flight, or freeze. I found myself swinging between these unhealthy responses as I grappled with my place in the world.

Fight response. The fight response is the defensiveness that flares up and refuses to acknowledge that I have more power and privilege in this world than others.[5] I carry a passport that allows me to come and go easily from almost any country in the world and gives me greater power than others who can't easily move around. In much of Africa and Asia, certain skin colors and nationalities are believed to have more authority, which is a privilege from which I directly benefit. I didn't earn this privilege, but I have it. I didn't seek it out, but I can't escape it. If I'm honest, I will admit that my first response to new information about the history of race and injustice tends toward the fight response. I'm a slow and stubborn learner, I guess.

Flight response. The flight response, by contrast, is the act of ignoring—burying our heads in the sand when we're confronted with the world's needs. But whenever we withdraw, whenever we turn our backs and walk away from the global poor, we walk away from Jesus himself.

Freeze response. Finally, many who want to engage cross-culturally are paralyzed by the fear of getting it wrong. The freeze response is characterized by guilt and inertia. It's that paralyzing sense of frustration that keeps me from engaging with the poor because I'm no longer allowed to engage on the terms that I had always imagined. The books and movies I consumed growing up, where (mostly) white saviors swooped in and saved the day, are now seen in a new, less flattering light. There's grief and shame over that because those people were my heroes growing up.

Each of these responses is also a form of denial. Each refuses to recognize that God is still calling us to be engaged—though perhaps not in the ways we had imagined.

As I thought about it, any of these three—fight, flight, or freeze—would not be a fruitful or mature response to the reality of my position in the world. My tears and enlightenment mean very little to those who have been sidelined and marginalized unless they are accompanied by wise action. As Desmond Tutu says, "If an elephant has its foot on the tail of a mouse and you say that you are neutral, the mouse will not appreciate your neutrality."[6]

I reminded myself that Jesus made it clear that we'd be judged harshly for taking the road of disengagement when he said, "Whatever you did not do for one of the least of these, you did not do for me" (Mt 25:45). If I were to move back overseas, I knew I had to find a way to engage with wisdom, courage, and humility. I had to identify the ways that injustice continues to thrive and, frankly, benefit people like me. Then I needed to redistribute that power, even at my own expense.

Jesus was calling me to move beyond both fight and freeze by engaging with the world on new and different terms. Global peace and justice—the kingdom of God on earth as it is in heaven (Mt 6:10)—cannot be achieved by any one race or group of people. Our destinies are inextricably tied together.

THE BASIC COMMISSION

When I broached the idea of returning to Cambodia with Nay, we smiled to think that our buddy Kevin was already there, immersing himself in a local community and trying to find his way as an outsider. Nay is a Cambodian-New Zealander, so you might think she leaped at the chance to return to the place of her birth, but she was hesitant as well—though for different reasons.

As a white man moving through the world and navigating life in Cambodia, I was used to being welcomed with open arms and wide smiles. Opportunities naturally flowed in my direction, and I was often pushed into a white savior role without even trying.

When Nay and I had visited local churches in Cambodia together, the local pastor would rush over to greet me and lead me by the arm to the front pew. He might even invite me to preach the sermon right there and then. Meanwhile, Nay would be left to fend for herself, dismissed because of her ethnicity and gender. This scene, repeated over and over again throughout our initial seven years in Cambodia, captured in a snapshot the difference between being a white male missionary and a non-white local believer. One was thrust into the role of star of the movie while the other was always an extra.

I wanted to give Nay space to consider the call and to hear from God for herself. I knew she wouldn't make the decision based on how easy or difficult the future might be; she had resisted choosing comfortable options for her entire life. But I knew this decision would cost her far more than it would cost me.

As we prayed and talked about how to serve cross-culturally as outsiders, we both wanted to be part of a new era of crosscultural servants who were seeking wisdom and insight instead of the limelight. Shortly after one of these conversations, Nay sat me down and looked at me with searching eyes. "I think we should move back to Cambodia." I knew she was right. We were being called to live our lives for God, no matter where he called us: to go into all the world, including our own neighborhood; to take crossing the oceans as seriously as crossing the street; and to respond to God's guidance, regardless of the cost, or the obstacles.

After months of cancer treatment and surgeries, I was given the green light by my doctors. And we began to prepare for the move back to the place and calling we thought we'd left behind. To a city we'd already bid farewell. And to a people we loved dearly. We were ready to discover a new way of serving as outsiders.

2

FROM APOSTLE (INSIDER) TO CATALYST (OUTSIDER)

Go to the people. Live with them. Learn from them.
Love them. Start with what they know. Build with what
they have. But with the best leaders, when the work
is done, the task accomplished, the people will say,
"We have done this ourselves."

LAO TZU

NAY WAS FIVE YEARS OLD WHEN HER MOTHER, fearing for the lives of her family under the brutal Khmer Rouge regime in Cambodia, flagged down a passing truck and slipped the driver her precious savings—twenty dollars—to hitch a ride. Twenty dollars to save their lives—a worthy deal.

The shirtless trucker, a cigarette dangling from his mouth, jumped down from the rusty blue cab and ambled to the back of the vehicle. As he untied the tarpaulin, a foul stench hit them with full force. Squinting, they peered into the dark pit—a steamy truckload of rich, dark excrement—and realized that for the next few hours, they would be nestled in the moist comfort of a fertilizer truck. Crap. The perfect hiding place!

Nay's motley band of survivors eventually traversed the Cambodian jungle into Thailand, avoiding landmines and child soldiers, to reach a refugee camp, where they received the welcome news that they had been accepted for relocation to New Zealand.

Thirty-five years later, we were back in Cambodia together again. A couple of months after our arrival, we found a promising community, a tiny tin-roof slum that was tucked away down an alley, a rabbit warren of shacks built on the edge of a sewer canal that was just a stone's throw from Victory Creek, where we had lived a decade before. We rented a two-bedroom house for our little family of four and moved in.

There's something about the most extreme places on earth that draws people like me, those with an entrepreneurial gifting or apostolic impulse. I guess we're drawn to adventure and newness. The earliest apostles had this adventurous spirit too. The apostle Paul was shipwrecked three times, thrown into prison, beaten with sticks, pelted with rocks, and still he kept pushing forward into new territories (2 Cor 11:21-29).

Apostles are gifted by God to establish new things in new places. The Greek word for apostle (*apostolos*) literally means "one who is sent," because apostles are sent out ahead of the pack, to push out kingdom boundaries and keep the church from turning inward. I didn't like this label, but I knew I was wired this way. So where does someone with an apostolic impulse start?

PIONEERING BEGINS WITH THE POOR

Not long after we moved into our little tin-roof house, I was swinging on my hammock in the front room as a handful of local kids played with LEGO bricks and books. Among them was one of my daughter's new Cambodian friends, a lively five-year-old girl named Roxy (her full name, Srey Rokesy, literally translates as "working girl").

Roxy's mother, like many of our neighbors, worked nights in the sordid underbelly of Phnom Penh's karaoke bars. She was forced to entertain the worst types of men—those who were flush with a little cash, red-faced with alcohol, and looking for cheap thrills. By tracing who was related to whom, we worked out that several families in our little slum village, including Roxy's family, represented at least three generations of prostitution and exploitation. It was a disturbing situation for a little girl who had done nothing but be born in the wrong place at the wrong time.

Perched on one of our wooden pallet-seats, Roxy fidgeted, bounced up and down, twirled her hair, chatted, and giggled over the picture books we had laid out. She looked up from a book she was examining and whispered a secret. "My *mak* [mother] lost her money gambling with cards last night," she confided. "Then she sold the baby clothes."

"What baby clothes?" I prompted, my heart sinking, as she went back to her book.

"You know . . . the baby clothes! For the new baby."

Roxy's mother was eight months pregnant, the father unknown. My heart broke for this struggling family. The biblical term *fatherless* took on a new shade of meaning for me that day.

Our interpretation of Scripture is determined by our context—where we live and what we see every day. If we read Scripture while sitting in a soft, upholstered chair in an affluent church building, the Bible will speak to us one way. But if we read Scripture in a grimy slum community, surrounded by kids like Roxy, that same Scripture will take on new meaning. It'll resonate at a deeper, more holistic level because the message of God is, at its core, "good news to the poor" (Lk 4:18). All our theology, whether we know it or not, is engaged either for or against the oppressed. We're either living as good news to the poor or we're not.

Reading the Ephesians framework for ministry while living alongside kids like Roxy and the many other fatherless children in that slum reinforced a conviction that had been growing within me for a long time. Surely God is calling *all* of us to serve the exploited and oppressed of the world through our unique gifts.[1] As Paul says when he introduces these ministry types,

> Christ himself gave the apostles, the prophets, the evangelists, the pastors and teachers, to equip his people for works of service [*diakonia*], so that the body of Christ may be built up. (Eph 4:11-12)

I had read these words outside of contexts of poverty many times, and I'd always skipped over the purpose for all five of these gifts, which was "to equip . . . people for works of service." *Diakonia* is the Greek word used for works of service. The way I'd always been taught, we jumped straight into using our gifts to build up the body of Christ. I skipped the *diakonia*! But in

27

doing so, I had missed the heart of this passage, which is that the body of Christ is established *first* through works of service—and especially for the poor and needy. In skipping that crucial part of the mission and vision of the church, it was natural to drift toward a narrower spiritual interpretation.

When our own physical needs are already met, we tend to limit our works of service to meeting spiritual needs. But when we focus on people's spiritual needs alone, the desperate physical, economic, political, and social needs of the majority of the world fade into the background. This passage becomes one more recipe for a type of evangelism and church planting that is hyperspiritualized rather than holistic. But God is interested in every aspect of our lives.

For example, Acts 6 recounts the story of the first apostles being confronted by community members who are concerned about the tangible needs of single moms and widows. The apostles saw that the *diakonia* (making sure that these struggling women had enough food on their tables) was not being properly fulfilled, so they pioneered a new structure (like good catalysts do!) and appointed new leaders of this ministry to care for needy mothers.

How many churches and denominations have overhauled their entire leadership structure and discipleship journey to implement the fivefold gifts of ministry (which are commonly referred to as APEST)[2] and yet overlooked the very first objective of equipping God's people, which is to serve the poor and needy? Jesus gave us apostles who would catalyze new works that would transform the lives of the poor and oppressed in order to build up the body of Christ. Simply put, the church must first be on the side of the poor because God himself has chosen to side with the poor and defenseless. Or to put it more provocatively, no one enters the kingdom without a letter of reference from the poor.

THE PROBLEM WITH BENEVOLENT OUTSIDERS

The first apostles, the ones who sat at Jesus' feet and received their teaching directly from the Big Boss himself, were so serious about their radical new way of life that they pioneered new communities of believers, who sold their possessions—their actual investment portfolios, holiday homes, and townhouses—and then redistributed cold, hard cash to the needy (Acts 2:45). Incredibly, they managed to eradicate economic poverty in their midst through this commitment to overcoming injustice (Acts 4:34-35). What an amazing accomplishment!

But don't forget that these apostles were operating within their own communities, with their own neighbors, families, and friends. They were insiders. Even Paul served within his own cultural sphere.[3] As a Roman citizen, he pioneered new work inside the Roman Empire. He didn't need to learn any new languages because he used Greek, and perhaps a smattering of Aramaic on occasion—languages he already knew well. In the Bible, apostles are almost always insiders. They pioneer within their own context.

As I grappled with this insight, I wondered what my apostolic gifting might look like in a crosscultural setting—one where I was an outsider with access to a lot more resources. As a gifted initiator, I am wired to respond to situations with an entrepreneurial fix-it-now mentality. I am dissatisfied with the status quo and want to jump in and solve problems immediately myself. I want to initiate! But I knew from my own bitter experiences in the past that jumping in as a benevolent outsider is the worst thing I can do; it leads directly to these mistakes:

Stifling local creativity.[4] When a community believes that the solutions to their problems will only come from outsiders instead of from within, they are robbed of the opportunity to find creative solutions themselves. This is tragic because there are few things as beautiful, empowering, and encouraging as a marginalized community coming together to solve a problem creatively themselves.

Weakening local self-esteem. Communities that are constantly on the receiving end of outside assistance come to believe that they have nothing to offer and begin to internalize the "beneficiary" or "victim" label that has been stuck on them by well-meaning outsiders. This is not only devastating to their sense of self, but it's also not the truth because economically poor communities are ridiculously rich in many other ways. They have a great deal to bring to the table.

Undermining local ownership. When outsiders take a strong lead in solving problems, the local people (insiders) will not fully own those outside solutions. Local ownership is crucial for the ongoing success and sustainability of any project. Otherwise, it'll slowly fizzle out after the outsiders leave.

Bypassing local resources. When large financial gifts come from outside a community, the tiny gifts that local people have to offer seem insignificant. Local believers ask themselves, "Why should I give toward this church building? My offering is chicken feed compared to what the foreigner brings." This causes them to redirect their energy toward finding outside benefactors instead of seeing their own contributions as important.

Creating unintended political alignments. When certain people in the community (such as those who speak English) are aligned with wealthy outsiders, their power and influence increase, and they are perceived as having access to resources. This is why you sometimes see non-Western pastors posting photos of themselves with foreign donors on their church walls (or Facebook newsfeeds).

Spurring false conversions. When missionaries are seen as a bridge to outside wealth and resources, it begins to look like a savvy investment to become a Christian. The unintended message to the wider community is that joining the church is a smart way to get goodies—jobs, cash, and Christmas shoeboxes. Some local people may participate just as long as the benefits last, whereas others may be suspicious of anyone who joins because they may see converts as the hirelings of foreigners.

These are some of the mistakes I made when I jumped in as a benevolent outsider in my apostolic endeavors, but I was now grappling with how those who have an apostolic calling might serve as "outsider catalysts" instead. A catalyst understands that God has already called local apostolic leaders to lead the way. The catalyst's role encourages these leaders to pioneer, helps them discern the way forward, and ensures that they truly own any new initiative. For true ownership, these local pioneers should be involved from the very earliest stages of anything new.

▼ THE CATALYST ◢

Catalysts are those who see the potential of insiders, recognize big-picture patterns, and work with locals to spark new ideas and explore new frontiers. They know that Christ is already at work in the local community—and began working long before they arrived. By God's grace, catalysts help local leaders draw those existing pieces together to create something new that they can own.

Seeing the Need

One day I was exploring further down the lane that ran alongside the sewer canal in our slum community, and I spotted a rundown hotel with a swimming pool. It was built on the edge of an overpass and separated from the surrounding slums by a concrete wall and barbed wire. Obviously, it was no Ritz Carlton.

I walked up to the front desk and asked the clerk, "Say, if I were to bring a small group of kids here for a swim, would that be possible?" I drummed my fingers on the counter.

"I guess we could do that, sir, but you'd need to pay since you're not a guest."

We negotiated a small fee, and I waltzed back home with a big grin on my face. "Nay! Let's take the neighborhood kids swimming. It'll be so nice for them to get out of the slum and do something healthy for a change."

Ever the realist, Nay was concerned. "None of these kids can swim. Come on, Craig, that sounds dangerous!"

In fact, two kids had tragically drowned in the thick, black water of the sewer canal the previous year just trying to find a place to play. Across Cambodia, the annual flood waters were a constant drowning danger for small children. In the end, we settled on taking a group of ten kids. If all went well, we could go back each week and teach more of them to swim.

The big day arrived, and the kids were pumped with excitement. Roxy grinned and made swimming strokes in the air. Soon, we were marching down the lane toward the hotel, a ragtag band of singing children dressed in tattered shorts and dirty T-shirts.

When we barged into the hotel foyer, the receptionist's mouth dropped open. "Oh, sorry, sir. You can't come in here like that."

I wondered what "like that" meant since I had only been in there a few days before, and I'd been welcomed with smiles. "I'm here to use the pool with my children and their friends," I ventured.

We were quickly ushered outside and around the back through the parking garage. The guard gave us a wink and grin as he pointed us to the pool. Some of the kids broke into a sprint and leaped into the water, fully clothed. Others held back, terrified. Roxy grabbed my hand. Before long, everyone was enjoying a raucous swim in the clean water.

As I lounged in the shallow end, trying to keep kids from climbing onto my head and shoulders, I realized that in the pandemonium, a crowd of children had gathered on the other side of the concrete wall from among the slum shacks. They were craning their necks to see and calling through the barbed wire to their friends on the inside. It struck me as a poignant and depressing picture of this world. So many are stuck in poverty, shut outside by the walls we've erected to protect the affluence and comfort of a few lucky ones.

As I pondered these thoughts, I noticed that some of the kids outside were surreptitiously hoisting their siblings over the wall into the pool area, using bits of clothing to protect them from the barbed (razor) wire. I was shocked, but I couldn't help laughing. I began to get up half-heartedly to tell them to stop. Then I thought, *Ah screw it*, and sat down with a chuckle and a glance at the guard, who seemed determined to look the other way.

When we left the pool that day, its water was a little dirtier, but our smiles were as bright as the sun.

IDENTIFYING LOCAL APOSTLES

Early the next morning, three little heads peeked into our doorway. "Can we go swimming again today, Uncle Craig?"

"No, not today, sorry. Next week, I promise!"

As they scampered off, an idea was brewing, so I picked up my phone and called Serey and Phearom, the local leaders of the Alongsiders movement. Serey was a quiet, strong woman in her midtwenties who wore her long hair pulled back in a ponytail. She had grown up in a Phnom Penh slum herself and had left a job as a cleaner to lead this vibrant youth movement. Phearom, a young man with wise eyes, wore jeans, sneakers, and a different *Star Wars* T-shirt every day. He had a hilarious sense of humor and a passion to come alongside young people, but his quick smile belied a painful past. Together, they made a formidable pair of young leaders.

During our previous years in Cambodia, we'd all worked together to mobilize hundreds of young Cambodian Christians to make a simple, but powerful, commitment to walk alongside one child each from their own communities. These young people aged sixteen to twenty-nine, called Alongsiders, would choose one vulnerable child to disciple as a "little brother" or "little sister." Incredibly, the movement had resonated with local churches, and numbers had continued to grow under Serey and Phearom's leadership while we had been living in Canada.

Since returning to Cambodia, I'd continued to meet with these gifted young Alongsiders regularly to encourage them and help spread the movement into other countries. Now we were sitting in a room in the Alongsiders office, talking again about the needs of vulnerable children across Cambodia. Roxy and my neighbors were heavy on my mind.

"Remember the last Alongsiders camp?" I grimaced. "How we rented that dingy old hotel, and they wouldn't let us use the hotel pool because they thought we might disrupt the other guests?"

Serey nodded, "I remember all the other guests—the tourists wearing bikinis around the pool. Our kids had never seen anything like that—it was so uncomfortable and weird!"

I'd forgotten that part of the story, but I knew that most rural Cambodians were very modest and would never wear a swimsuit, let alone a bikini.

Serey chimed in again, "Yeah, it wasn't easy holding a camp for our Alongsiders and their little brothers and sisters at that hotel. The food was so expensive! Remember how we had to pile all four hundred kids onto buses for every single lunch and dinner so we could find cheaper places to eat across town? What a pain."

She gave a wistful smile. "Imagine if we had our own campsite—now that would be amazing! A place for all the kids of Cambodia—somewhere schools, orphanages, and churches could use. No more dingy hotels!"

Later, I found Phearom sitting on the curb outside, deep in thought. I sat down beside him and said, "What are you thinking, Phearom?"

"I've had this idea brewing for a kind of boot camp for a long time," he said softly. "I want to take young people on a deep discipleship journey," he continued, his voice rising with excitement. "I want them to discover God and discover who God made them to be—but we need to get them out into nature to do that."

"That's truly a beautiful vision, Phearom."

Phearom went on to explain how he was already taking small groups of young people from his church into the wilderness for camps. I realized that Phearom was a spiritual pioneer at heart. He had a history of starting new initiatives and gathering people around him. He was a local apostle—a true innovator from among his own people.

Exploring the Biblical Foundations

I went home and reread Acts 2, a passage that had resonated with me from our Vancouver days. I sensed that it might be significant in this season of birthing something new.

They devoted themselves to the apostles' teaching and to fellowship, to the breaking of bread and to prayer.

Everyone was filled with awe at the many wonders and signs performed by the apostles. All the believers were together and had everything in common. They sold property and possessions to give to anyone who had need. Every day they continued to meet together in the temple courts. They broke bread in their homes and ate together with glad and sincere hearts, praising God and enjoying the favor of all the people. And the Lord added to their number daily those who were being saved. (Acts 2:42-47)

What struck me about this description was how utterly foreign it felt in contrast to the way most believers live today. We're just not that devoted to daily teaching and prayer.

I thought back to church in Canada. Fellowship was a coffee before church once a week, if that. We rarely shared our possessions with each other, except maybe the Netflix password— and even that was reserved for family members. Most of us were not eating dinner together regularly or spending time praising God together outside of a Sunday morning. That's why we had started our open table in the Downtown Eastside. Honestly, most Christians just aren't experiencing the kind of Christian community that those early apostles pioneered,[5] but as I read Acts in our tiny slum house in Cambodia, I was inspired all over again.

As I pondered this lack of community in the lives of believers, I knew that there was one exception. In the average believer's life, there is perhaps one time a year when most Christians have the chance to experience that depth of community—and that's the experience of going away for camp. I figured that if the hopes and dreams of Serey and Phearom were to be fulfilled, they would be able to take hundreds of Alongsiders youth and their little brothers and sisters to camp. For just a few days, the Alongsiders would eat all their meals together, in fellowship around cheap plastic tables. For a few brief days, they would live together in dorm rooms, and they would all use the same camp plates, cups, and cutlery. They would even share bathrooms!

And during camp, both rich and poor would live together at the same economic level. There would be no more concrete walls with barbed wire separating the haves from the have-nots. Everyone would sleep on the same simple beds. In the early church community, "No one claimed that any of their possessions was their own, but they shared everything they had" (Acts 4:32). Moreover, there were "no needy persons among them" (Acts 4:34). I thought that this same ethos could be reflected in the camp that Phearom and Serey were imagining. This would not be communism but a taste of radical, upside-down kingdom living on a short-term basis. It would be "subversive camping."

For just a few days, everyone would receive a depth of regular teaching and worship that would light their hearts on fire. Sitting around the camp bonfire would be the perfect metaphor for the newly lit flame of spiritual passion. Those of us who had been to camps in the West often came home on spiritual highs, feeling closer to God and each other. But for the Alongsiders and their little brothers and sisters, something even deeper could occur. They would go back home to a deeper discipleship relationship that would continue through the rest of the year.

At camp, they could begin to catch a vision for how to live counter-culturally in a world that teaches us to hoard our snacks and withdraw into our Netflix nests. At camp, they could imagine ways to simplify their lifestyles so that the needy might be welcomed around the feasting table, and their time could be freed up to focus on the things of God. For just a few days, everyone at camp could glimpse the kind of Christian community that Jesus meant for us to experience on a daily basis.

Perhaps the light-handed touch of a catalyst could help these local leaders bring their dream for Cambodia's first-ever adventure camp for kids to fruition—a place of healing and laughter, feasting and fun. As I reflected on Serey and Phearom's dream, a phrase from my past popped into my mind: "Cook too much food. Invite too many people."

3

DANGER #1
POWER

*The white savior supports brutal policies in the morning,
founds charities in the afternoon, and receives awards
in the evening. The White Savior Industrial Complex is not
about justice. It is about having a big emotional
experience that validates privilege.*

TEJU COLE

PHEAROM HAD A BRUTAL CHILDHOOD. He was born as an identical twin in the dusty, provincial Cambodian town of Battambang, and his father died of cancer when he and his brother were only three months old.

Following traditional Cambodian cultural practices, Phearom's mother consulted a local fortuneteller to figure out the cause of her husband's death. This fortuneteller informed Phearom's mother that he and his brother, Phearak, were a double curse—unlucky twins—who were surely responsible for their father's death. After hearing this, Phearom's mother could barely stand to be around her twin sons, so she decided to place them in an orphanage.

Once Phearom and Phearak reached the age when they could work (about six or seven years old), Phearom's aunt decided to adopt the boys and use them as household helpers. Their lonely and bewildering life suddenly became even more difficult as they were subjected to daily beatings and abuse by their aunt and uncle.

Then one day, when Phearom was eight, as he tried to scramble away from the fists raining down on his head, he fell from the window of the house onto the ground, where he lay unconscious in the dirt. Phearom spent the next weeks in a coma, lying on a forgotten bed in the corner of a bare room in the provincial hospital. His condition worsened, and after three months, the doctor, who only had access to primitive equipment, declared Phearom dead.

The hospital contacted Phearom's aunt and uncle to see if they wished to have him cremated at the hospital or to bring him home for the customary Khmer ceremony. After a brief discussion, they told the hospital to deal with the body, complaining that the cost had already been too high, and there was no money for a funeral. So Phearom's body was moved to the morgue to be readied for cremation.

The next day, when the time for the cremation arrived, there were no tearful relatives or friends to say farewell to this little boy, who had known nothing but pain. His twin brother grieved at home, not allowed to visit the hospital.

The hospital orderly rolled Phearom's body out from the freezer on a gurney and prepared to ready the body for its final resting state. *Ashes to ashes. Dust to dust.*

As the orderly pulled back the sheet, he noticed a slight twitch out of the corner of his eye. He stared intently at the cadaver, feeling his own pulse pounding in the silence. As he stared at Phearom's corpse, the walls seemed to close in around him. Then he saw a tiny wiggle in Phearom's fingers. The orderly ran from the room, shrieking in terror, "The body is moving! The body is moving!"

Led by a courageous doctor, hospital staff crowded into the room, first pushing forward and then shrinking back as they witnessed the barely perceptible twitch in Phearom's fingers. The doctor lowered his head to Phearom's chest, held his hand up in the air for silence, and listened intently. "There's a heartbeat!" the doctor shouted. "He's alive! Bring him upstairs."

Though Phearom's life was snatched from the clutches of flames and death, he had to return to his aunt's house, where the daily cycle of school, work, and beatings continued. He and his brother never imagined that their life could get any better, but when they were fifteen, they moved into a children's center, where the beatings and work ceased, and they were able to concentrate on their education. Then everything changed in their late teens, when they became followers of Jesus through the outreach of a local church, and they began to experience new life and resurrection in an even deeper way.

One day at church, Phearom heard about the Alongsiders vision to reach out and walk alongside vulnerable children, and it immediately captivated his heart. Phearom had known intimately what it was like to be neglected and abused, and he also knew what a difference it would have made to have had an Alongsider looking out for him when he was growing up scared and alone.

Full of excitement, Phearom went to his pastor with a proposal to form a group at their church. To his disappointment, his pastor turned him down. Not accustomed to giving up easily, Phearom gathered a number of wayward kids from the local village and committed to disciple them himself. If no one would join him, he would lead the way alone until others caught on! Phearom's efforts to disciple local youth eventually bore fruit, and he gained the trust and admiration of his pastor as more and more youth began joining the church and growing in faith. As soon as we met Phearom, we recognized him as a natural leader, so we invited him to take on a leadership role within the Alongsiders movement.

For much of Phearom's life, he was at the mercy of malevolent power players who claimed that he was a curse. Those who abandoned him when he was so vulnerable and those who abused him to the point of near death had wielded power in ways that had hurt Phearom. The danger for Phearom was that he would simply exchange malevolent power players for benevolent power players. While benevolence is better than malevolence, the subtle danger for most catalysts is to use a position of power over those who are marginalized or oppressed for "good" rather than discerning how to empower and strengthen them.

THE DANGER OF STORYTELLING[1]

From *The Blind Side* to *Avatar, Green Book* to *The Help,* Hollywood loves a white savior—and so do we. All these movies are variations on the same cliché: the white savior arrives, sympathizes with the problems of the people, learns what needs to happen to solve their problems, wins their favor, and becomes the hero.

We see this in nonfiction as well—*Kony, Three Cups of Tea, Kisses from Katie,* and many more. These charity stories reflect our appetite for narratives that place outsiders in the middle of an insider story.

The problem with this white savior way of telling a story is that the people whom God places at the center of their own transformation—local leaders, such as Phearom—are relegated to the margins. Local people become bit players in the story of a great foreign hero. When we come with power and privilege into fragile situations of poverty, such as the village where Phearom grew up with his family and neighbors, we risk undermining local solutions if we are not self-aware and self-disciplined.

The narrative of poor people as pathetic victims has been spread far and wide by those who want to mobilize more missionaries and raise more funds. And for good reason: people take action when they feel like their engagement will bring change. But the tide is shifting. Wiser organizations and communicators are realizing that portraying the poor as pathetic, helpless victims is not especially helpful—nor truthful.

Recognizing this problem, I wondered how we could help Phearom tell his own story with integrity. After getting to know him better, I invited him to make a short video about the story of his life to inspire other Alongsiders leaders around the world. He was so excited to have the chance to tell his story in his own words.[2]

We each have a role to play in this broken world, but when God calls us to serve, God isn't asking us to become outsider heroes in the middle of an insider's story. God is already the hero, and God is inviting us to walk alongside local insiders as sidekicks rather than as superheroes. Our role is to amplify the voices of local leaders, to strengthen their hands, and to place them at the front and center.

If you are a caring person who gives a rip about injustice, there are times when you'll be called to communicate the truth about situations of injustice and poverty to your friends, your church, and within your sphere of influence. You can and should be an advocate. As one local activist put it, "Use your liberty to promote ours."

But how do we speak of poverty without being a jerk? How do we speak of injustice without playing the great white superhero role? Patrisse Cullors, a young black leader, helpfully articulates the following approach:

> I think it's important in this current historical moment that we're naming the tragedy and the resilience. So, the tragedy is black people are being killed often and continue to be killed often. The tragedy is that black people are living in poverty. Black folks have the highest rate of

homelessness. Those are the tragedies, but there is this—also this other side, which is this amazing movement that is challenging age-old racism and discrimination. And I always tell audiences what a great time to be alive, to show up for this current historical moment.[3]

As Cullors observes, both the tragedy and the resilience are important and true.

Her words have helped me see that if I describe only the tragedy, such as the abuse that Phearom suffered, or the poverty he faced, or the injustice he endured, I would be casting him as a pathetic victim who could do nothing but wait for an outside savior like me to come along and provide all the answers. I would end up framing the response to poverty and injustice around myself and the money I could raise.

Once again, mammon would become the savior of the world, the very thing Jesus so carefully warned us against (Mt 6:24). In falling into this trap, nonprofit organizations become huge fundraising and marketing operations.

Of course, fundraisers might be slicker and less condescending nowadays, but the essential narrative hasn't changed much—donors and their money are the change makers of the world. Yay for rich people—the saviors of poor people! When we name only the tragedy, we deny the work that God is already doing in the lives of local people, such as Phearom, and their communities.

On the flip side, if I name only the resilience—describing only how brave and strong and clever Phearom has been in overcoming his problems and becoming a leader—I would be glossing over the very real challenges that he has faced and the struggles he continues to overcome. I would end up romanticizing the lives of the marginalized and caricaturing them as "the happy poor." When we name only the resilience, we ignore our own complicity in an unjust system. We deny the invitation that God extends to us to repent and come alongside those who are poor and oppressed.

When we talk only about the resilience of the poor and oppressed, we presume that they are 100 percent responsible for solving all the problems that they face—so that we can get back to our comfortable lifestyles with a relieved sigh. When we name only their resilience, apathy reigns supreme, and we miss the beautiful invitation to come alongside young leaders like Phearom and encourage their strengths and empower them to use these strengths for good in their own local communities.

I knew that if Phearom were going to tell his story, he would need to hold both the tragedy and the resilience in creative tension. And those who would hear his story would need to sense an invitation to embrace inspiration rather than guilt.

PLAYING GOD

The ancient Cambodian proverb "It takes a spider to repair its own web" offers an insightful image for what we are trying to achieve in Alongsiders because the spider, the insider, is the key player. Local people must be at the heart of what God is doing in any particular place. Our role as catalysts and outsiders is to come alongside them and to strengthen what they are already doing. As outsiders, we are called to amplify their voices, lighten their loads, and equip and support them, for in the long run, leaders such as Phearom will be the true change makers in their communities—not us.

As the ancient words of the prophet Isaiah remind us,

> *Your* people will rebuild the ancient ruins
>   and will raise up the age-old foundations;
> *You* will be called Repairer of Broken Walls,
>   Restorer of Streets with Dwellings. (Is 58:12,
>   emphasis added)

This passage highlights the power of God's Spirit as it is revealed through the resilience and actions of insiders.

The greatest danger for a catalyst—and indeed any outsider—is to play God in the lives of the poor. This is a form of idolatry, by which we steal the authority and power that belong to God alone and take them for ourselves.

In Sunday school, I learned that God has three key attributes: omniscience (all-knowing), omnipotence (all-powerful), and omnipresence (everywhere). What I didn't learn in Sunday school is that these attributes also describe the most common ways that benevolent outsiders attempt to take on the role of God in the lives of those with whom they are working.[4]

THE OMNISCIENCE TRAP

The first way we fall into playing God is by acting as if we know everything—or at least more than we actually do. Psychologists call this the Dunning-Kruger Effect[5]—a cognitive bias that causes people with limited knowledge or competence to greatly underestimate their lack of understanding. Cultural outsiders do this all the time, especially in their early years of service.

Of course, most of us don't admit that we are know-it-alls (even if everyone else around may perceive us in this way). But in resource-poor situations, expertise is often conferred on outsiders just because of the color of their skin or their passport. In these situations, you may have an eighteen-year-old from England on a gap year teaching science at a Kenyan high school, or you may have a lawyer from the United States constructing a house in Mexico.

Of course, we should have a healthy awareness of any expertise we bring into a situation—if we do, in fact, bring along any expertise in a particular area. But unfortunately, we often don't realize what we *don't* know. This makes the posture of humility and listening crucial for outsiders.

This point was driven home to me when we visited another building project just outside the city to get ideas for our camp. A group of well-meaning Christians from Western countries had come to "bless" poor Cambodians by building them houses. Each of the houses had been built with a solid tile roof and concrete block walls, a cute front door, and a brass plaque on the front, stating who had worked hard to come and build it. To my eyes, they looked smart.

The only problem was that poor Cambodians generally build their houses on stilts so they can sit underneath them during the heat of the day and enjoy the cool breeze. Without money to install air conditioning, this lifestyle in the shade helps them to survive the stifling heat of Cambodia's long hot season.

Because no one wanted to live in these ill-conceived foreign monstrosities, they stood empty and abandoned on the edge of the village—a testament to another failed outsider intervention, and the omniscience trap. A stone's throw away stood an abandoned water pump and well that had been installed by a different group of foreigners. These had also fallen into disrepair and lay unused, rusting away.[6]

Without local consultation, insights, and expertise, the results of both interventions were a sad failure. Of course, the short-term missionaries in each group most likely had good hearts, and all of them were probably deeply impacted by their trip and went back to their home churches bursting with amazing tales of miracles and encouragement. But good intentions are not enough. Their efforts had fallen into the omniscience trap.

To combat this problem, we need to invest enough time in a place and a culture to understand how much we simply do not know. The Dunning-Kruger Effect reduces over time as we learn more and become more familiar with the situation. So, the simplest answer to the omniscience trap is time. Years, in fact.

THE OMNIPRESENCE TRAP

In contrast, the second way we fall into playing God is by sticking around too long and never stepping back to let local people lead. We are omnipresent—always there, always chipping in our two cents worth, always hovering.

I spent time with Phearom and other local leaders to dream about what it might look like to create something new together, something that would grow out of the Cambodian soil and be a source of hope and shalom for Cambodian children. As a catalyst, I needed a great deal of self-discipline to avoid overstepping my role in encouraging Phearom and the other leaders in developing the camp. This is especially true in cultures where people are naturally more soft-spoken and relational. In Cambodia, folks will defer to the foreigner nine times out of ten. When, from time to time, I found myself raising my voice and saying, "Just get it done!" I knew I'd blown it once again.

We turned to Luke 9, where Jesus gathers his team together for an inspiring chat about missions. Jesus wanted to send them out to do some ministry, so he gave them power and authority to go out and kick some demon butt and heal some sick people. Then Jesus gave them one final instruction: he commanded his team, "Whatever house you enter, stay there until you leave that town" (Lk 9:4).

It seems that Jesus knew there was an ideal length of time to remain in each place—neither too short, nor too long. This is why we need sensitivity to the Spirit and a sensitivity to the unspoken words of those we are serving alongside.

When I first moved to Cambodia, I would proudly tell people I'd be buried here on Cambodian soil. But, for me at least, those noble words were rooted in a certain pride and a lack of understanding. There is a time to step back. There is a time to give local leaders space. And there is a time to leave. Jesus' ministry, including growing up, was thirty-three years. Then Jesus took the biggest gamble of all—he stepped back and left it all in the hands of a team of unemployed fishermen, rejected bureaucrats, disreputable women, and some failed revolutionaries. If the antidote to the omniscience trap is time, the antidote to the omnipresence trap is trust.

THE OMNIPOTENCE TRAP

The third way we fall into playing God is by becoming a patron instead of pointing people to the true provider. This is a very real temptation because we almost always have access to vastly more resources than local folks.

Notice Jesus' instructions for the mission trip in Luke 9: "Take nothing for the journey—no staff, no bag, no bread, no money, no extra shirt" (Lk 9:3). Not even a change of undies?! This was seriously a challenging statement.

As our local team grappled with Jesus' words in Luke 9, we began to see that by stripping his team of the ability to meet their most basic needs, Jesus was forcing them to rely on God and the local resources of the people they visited. He was placing them in a posture of interdependence.

The antidote to the omnipotence trap is self-discipline. We simply must hold back from unleashing all our resources in each situation of need. It feels counterintuitive. It even feels terribly wrong sometimes. But look at Jesus . . .

Jesus was showing his team that local people would always need to be at the center of the transformation of their own communities so that they would look to God to meet their needs instead of to outsiders. Matthew put it even more clearly:

"Provide neither gold nor silver nor copper in your money belts, nor bag for your journey, nor two tunics, nor sandals, nor staffs; for a worker is worthy of his food" (Mt 10:9-10 NKJV).

We knew that this was an incredibly important posture for our works of service—and the very best way to trust God for the building of a camp. We sensed that we were being called to start this project with empty hands and to look to God together to meet the needs.

I already knew that bringing in a lot of outside resources, a strategy that the local people could not copy, would be not empowering but would be immensely disempowering because it would send the clear message that problems could be solved only by well-resourced outsiders. While outside resources might make an immediate difference and solve a problem for the time being, the next time the people faced a similar problem, they'd be forced to turn back to me (or some other white savior like me) for help, thus setting in motion the inevitable patron-client dependency that we all know and love to hate. Phearom was wisely thinking these things through for himself and coming to the same conclusions.

As our Alongsiders leadership team began to pray, we admitted that we had absolutely no money to buy land for an adventure camp. We also acknowledged that we lacked the technical expertise to build something that would last, nor did we have an architect to draw up the plans. Moreover, we didn't have the bandwidth to pioneer such a major project on our own since the Alongsiders movement was now growing rapidly into other countries.

We all knew it would take a miracle to pull off this vision because we were completely empty handed. We also knew that it would be an amazing journey in faith for all of us to trust God to bring this vision together in his time and his way.

You'd think the first disciples of Jesus would have learned this important principle by the time they got back from their first mission trip. They had been totally reliant on God for all their needs. They had taught reliance on God to the local people, and they had seen miracles. "When the apostles returned, they reported to Jesus what they had done. Then he took them with him and they withdrew by themselves to a town called Bethsaida, but the crowds learned about it and followed him" (Lk 9:10-11). But then they faced an even greater challenge. As they withdrew with Jesus for a little R & R after their first mission trip, they had to face a bunch of people sitting on a hillside with rumbling stomachs—at least five thousand of them. We already know what Jesus said to the disciples: "You give them something to eat" (Lk 9:13). Remember, the disciples had just gotten back from a trip where they were forbidden to carry food or cash; they certainly could not have been carrying the resources to feed five thousand people.

Those who complain that relying on God just doesn't work in the real world of massive needs might have a similar scenario in mind. And on the surface, Jesus' command to feed such a huge crowd must have seemed pretty ridiculous—unless you had been learning to see how God starts with the resources that local people already have.

Unfortunately, the lesson was still sinking in because the disciples seemed to scratch their heads, unable to grasp what Jesus was doing. Once again, Jesus patiently demonstrated the principle of local ownership and local resources, what today we would call Asset-Based Community Development (ABCD).[7]

Then a little boy approached and held up his offering, like a handful of tuna sandwiches, to get the ball rolling. In Alongsiders, we have learned, time and time again, that it's often the young and vulnerable, the very people who are overlooked, who have the faith to trust in God. I thought of Phearom, who had come from a background of absolute poverty and abuse. In the eyes of the world, he had little to offer, but in the eyes of God, he was a mighty leader—a leader who was willing to step forward and offer whatever he had.

Taking the boy's offering, Jesus blessed it, then the disciples began to see how the immediate need of feeding five thousand hungry people could be met in a way that anyone in the future could replicate—if only they had the eyes to see the resources that had already been given and the eyes of faith to trust in the abundance of a loving God. At the heart of this approach is our willingness to come before God with open hands and to look to God to meet our needs, just as Jesus did (Phil 2:7).

As we dreamed together about an adventure camp for Cambodian children, these gospel stories about vulnerability and trust in God shaped our prayers and discussions. Though we did not yet know how God would provide for the adventure camp, our faith was growing.

4

FROM PROPHET (INSIDER) TO ALLY (OUTSIDER)

The poor tell us who we are, and the prophets tell us who we could be, so we hide the poor, and kill the prophets.

PHILIP BERRIGAN

PHEAROM'S VOICE TREMBLED with excitement as he told me over the phone, "Craig, I think we've got a piece of land." He had found a twelve-acre parcel of bush and rice paddies nestled at the base of a mountain just outside the coastal town of Kep, three hours from Phnom Penh.

Phearom had already seen the land and was excited to show it to me and my father. Mum and Dad had recently relocated to Cambodia to help with the camp construction, just as they had helped construct schools and other building projects in Southeast Asia. As we hiked in the baking sun from the road to the top of the mountain, the real estate agent told us about the bloody history of the area.

In previous decades, Cambodian elites had taken their vacations in Kep, where they enjoyed the local seafood and built beautiful mansions along the coastline. But all that development came to a bloody end when the Vietnam War spilled over into Cambodia, and the US government began a secret bombing campaign. Nixon's chief of staff wrote in his diary that the final decision to carpet bomb Cambodia "was made at a meeting in the Oval Office Sunday afternoon, after the church service."[1]

Soon after that decision, in March 1969, the American government sent B-52 bombers to target Cambodian sites. Ultimately, more than two million tons of bombs were dropped on thousands of villages across Cambodia (fourteen times the blast force of the bombs dropped on Hiroshima and Nagasaki during World War II),[2] forcing a third of the Cambodian population to flee for their lives. This American campaign of terror gave Cambodia the dubious honor of being the most bombed country in the history of the world.[3]

Supposedly, the bombing was targeted at Vietnamese soldiers, the Viet Cong, who crossed back and forth over the border with Cambodia. Yet there was also a total disregard for civilian life, a tiptoe tyranny that came right from the top. As President Nixon ordered the national security adviser,[4] Henry Kissinger, at the time, "They have got to go in there and I mean really go in. I don't want the gunships, I want the helicopter ships. I want everything that can fly to go in there and crack the hell out of them. There is no limitation on mileage and there is no limitation on budget. Is that clear?"[5]

The result was absolute devastation and massive loss of life. One Cambodian eyewitness to the bombing described the event as follows: "Three F-111s bombed right in the middle of my village, killing eleven of my family members. My father was wounded but survived. At that time, there was not a single soldier in the village or in the area around the village. Twenty-seven other villagers were also killed. They had run into a ditch to hide and then two bombs fell right into it."[6]

Some estimate that half a million Cambodians were killed by these sorties, and many more were injured or permanently disabled. The carpet bombing continued until 1973. By that time, Cambodian villagers had been thoroughly politicized by the killing of their neighbors and family members. A tiny communist insurgency called the Khmer Rouge, which was led by Pol Pot, capitalized on the anger of ordinary Cambodians to recruit tens of thousands more to their revolutionary cause. As the American CIA's Directorate of Operations explained in a 1973 intelligence information cable,

> Khmer insurgent (KI) [Khmer Rouge] cadre have begun an intensified proselyting campaign among ethnic Cambodian residents . . . in an effort to recruit young men and women for KI military organizations. They are using damage caused by B-52 strikes as the main theme of their propaganda.[7]

This tactic worked. The Khmer Rouge swelled from fewer than ten thousand soldiers to more than two hundred thousand as a direct result of the American attacks. In 1975, Phnom Penh, the capital of Cambodia, fell to the Khmer Rouge, who then began a radical experiment in taking the country back to "Year

Zero." As the revolutionary troops swept into the city, they used loudspeakers to announce that another American bombing attack was imminent. They warned all residents to leave the city immediately. Phnom Penh was emptied, and the experiment began. Millions more died. The country was decimated.[8]

The twelve-acre parcel of land that we were considering for the adventure camp was situated at the base of a mountain that the locals called Hiding Place Mountain. As our team learned more about the history of the area, the name began to make sense. People from the surrounding villages had literally run for their lives to the hills, time and again, to escape the carnage of American fire power. Such atrocities continue to this day as US drones wreak havoc around the world.[9]

The land was overgrown with a wild and dense knot of lush green vegetation, but two huge coconut trees arose majestically from the green tangle. After hiking to the top of the slope, we took in the amazing view over the contours of the land—the rice and salt fields on the flats and the ocean sparkling in the distance.

I thought about the name of the mountain, Hiding Place, which had offered refuge to the fearful local people who had been through so much trauma. The land sloped gently down into a cozy valley, which had provided protection from the hail of American carpet bombs. I understood why people had hidden in this place of refuge and shelter, this sanctuary from war and violence. As we stood together and prayed on that parcel of land, a gentle breeze blew across our skin, and a great sense of peace filled our hearts.

"Phearom, this valley is filled with shalom," I murmured.

"Yes, I feel so peaceful here!" Phearom's eyes lit up as he smiled at me.

Addressing Injustice

Phearom and I began to meet with a small group of Cambodian Christian leaders who gathered each month to discuss the recent deterioration of human rights in the country. We searched Scripture to understand God's heart for the poor and for justice. My role was to accompany them in their Bible studies and to join them as they cried out to God, not to lead their efforts.

Each month, these leaders would share about the challenges they were facing with corruption, land-grabbing, or government surveillance. Some of them were involved in supporting villagers who were trying to protect the forests from illegal logging. They wanted to know what Jesus said about their situations.

At the same time, Phearom and other Khmer leaders in our movement were grappling with local authorities in Kep, who were demanding bribes for rezoning the land so that it could become a camp. These authorities were also giving them the runaround as our team tried to gain all the necessary building permits.

As we discussed all these challenges, I often thought back to my days in Vancouver, where we'd had the luxury of marching in the streets and camping out in front of various government agencies, creatively asking for basic human rights issues to be addressed. We had chained ourselves up outside an embassy to protest one country's then lack of legal protections for foreign workers. And we led a Pirates of Justice flash mob to protest the exploitation of staff on cruise ships that were docked in Vancouver's beautiful ports. We had welcomed press attention to our causes, and sometimes we had even seen breakthroughs.

But here in Cambodia there was an atmosphere of oppression and fear. My Cambodian friends spoke to me in whispers or checked who might be listening whenever they dared to speak about injustice. In our Bible study, they felt free to share openly, but the guest list was tightly controlled by my friend Mony, who had been the target of government surveillance. Mony's wisdom about how to deal with oppressive regimes guided all of us. "Those noisy protests you see in other countries won't work here," he warned. "They'll just crush you like a bug."

Mony's warning reminded me of a group of Cambodian women from one of the city slums who had become furious that their land was being stolen by government-backed developers to build condos. They had dragged their beds into the middle of Phnom Penh's busiest intersection and held up protest signs, saying they had nowhere else to go since their homes were the target of developers. They were immediately arrested and put on trial within twenty-four hours. With no chance for defense or a proper court case, they had been sentenced to a year in prison that same day.[10]

I realized that the prophetic gifting looks very different in a non-Western context—as do each of the other fivefold ministry gifts listed in Ephesians. I also knew that I personally felt called to take more prophetic action at times. Consequently, I wondered what God might be asking me to do in Cambodia, a more dangerous context than Vancouver.

Whenever we come into situations of injustice as outsiders with power and privilege, we must come as alongsiders. We must walk alongside local people, carefully seeking to use our power wisely. In most cases, we should not lead the charge toward justice, but we must come alongside the local people as allies so that we can strengthen their hands and amplify their voices.

▼ THE ALLY ◢

Allies know God's heart for the marginalized. These allies seek to come alongside the marginalized and use their privilege to amplify the many local voices that are struggling to be heard. Allies care deeply about justice and mercy, and they are bold enough to speak truth to power in situations of injustice— especially in their own circles of influence. As outsiders, allies are uniquely positioned to question the status quo and call the global community toward God's kingdom on earth, using their privilege (access, training, and resources) to support the causes championed by local people.

A wise ally will recognize that sometimes it will be too dangerous to amplify the voices of the oppressed. In fact, the oppressed may tell you to shut up when you try to amplify their voices because they don't want to be gunned down in broad daylight. So, should we speak up at all? Aren't we guests in these countries? Maybe we should just pipe down!

But when we remain silent in the face of injustice, our silence is still political. We are voting for the status quo to continue. We are saying, "Carry on with what you are doing. I will not rock the boat, no matter what you do to the poor and oppressed." Thus, our silence implicitly supports injustice.[11]

Twiddling our thumbs while any government mistreats refugees, minority ethnic groups, unborn children, or the children of the countries where our nation drops bombs is still a deeply political act. We cannot sit on the fence. As Dietrich Bonhoeffer said, "Silence in the face of evil is itself evil. God will not hold us guiltless. Not to speak is to speak. Not to act is to act."[12]

If Christians had been silent in the face of slavery, we might have never seen the successes of William Wilberforce and his band of abolitionists. If Christians had been silent in the face of segregation, we might never have seen the civil liberties for which Martin Luther King Jr. campaigned—and died.

As Cornel West says, "Justice is what love looks like . . . in public."[13] To do justice is to love our neighbors in public. When the poor are being crushed, the most ethical and Christlike response will be to stand up for them. When Christian activists speak out against injustice in creative ways, we are continuing a long biblical tradition of prophetic action that culminates with the life of Jesus.

This call to speak truth to power traces right back through the history of God's people. For example, the Old Testament activist, Isaiah, went around for three years, naked and barefoot, as a sign against Egypt and Cush (Is 20:2-6). He wanted to show his fellow countrymen that these two countries (nations in whom Israel had put their hope) would be led away into exile, naked and barefoot, by the Assyrians. This prophetic action vividly and shockingly challenged Israel's unjust foreign policy.

Another activist, Jeremiah, broke a clay jar at the valley of Ben Hinnom in front of some of the elite leaders of Jerusalem. His protest was a warning that God would soon shatter their people and city if they did not turn away from injustice (Jer 19:1-13).[14] Another activist named Nehemiah shook out the front of his garment as a dramatic piece of performance art, explaining to the people in Jerusalem that God would shake out from their houses those who did not turn away from exploitative lending practices (Neh 5:13).[15] All these are prophets. And Jesus himself had a bunch of acidic things to say about corrupt and crooked leaders, but we often gloss over his words, or we reframe them as "spiritual" because we don't understand the political situation of Judea during his time.

In 61 BC, all of Judea had been conquered by the oppressive Roman Empire. The Romans, who were basically absentee landlords, had delegated their power to local political leaders— a bunch of religious thugs and charlatans. The Roman governor was the most powerful political figure in Judea, and the senior pastor was Caiaphas, the high priest.

By the time Jesus came on the scene, the whole nation was in upheaval. Amid these turbulent times in Judea, four competing groups had risen to power and influence: the Sadducees, who sucked up to Rome and reaped the benefits; the Pharisees, who wanted to separate from Rome and form a religious state; the Zealots, who wanted to overthrow Rome with a well-regulated militia; and the Essenes, who were the hippies of their time and opted to live in communes.

The Sadducees, who were also known as the chief priests, had the most political power. They hugged the Romans in their sycophantic embrace, and this drove the Pharisees nuts. As a result of their bootlicking, the Sadducees were given political responsibility for all kinds of things: collecting taxes, equipping and leading the army, administering the state domestically, representing the state internationally, and regulating relations with the Romans. Thus, the Sadducees were some of the most powerful local politicians in the land. The Sadducees also controlled the temple, which was the very center of Jewish society and governance, so they held both religious and political clout. John the Baptist aggressively called the Sadducees a "brood of vipers" (Mt 3:7). Jesus called them "wicked" (Mt 16:1-5) and also accused them of being completely "wrong" on multiple issues (Mt 22:23-34 NRSV; Mk 12:18-27 NRSV).

But the Sadducees weren't the only ones with authority in Judea. In the Gospel of Mark, Jesus criticizes another group of local leaders known as the scribes or "teachers of the law." Jesus instructs his disciples to "watch out" for these "teachers of the law" (Mk 12:38) right before he points out the widow who puts her two small coins into the offering plate at the temple. Though the story about this woman is familiar, we often miss the way that Jesus singles her out to expose the corruption of these leaders who "devour widows' houses and for a show make lengthy prayers." Next, he says that "these men will be punished most severely" (Mk 12:40). After this scathing criticism, the narrative continues with the well-known story about the widow and her pennies:

> Jesus sat down opposite the place where the offerings were put and watched the crowd putting their money into the temple treasury. Many rich people threw in large amounts. But a poor widow came and put in two very small copper coins, worth only a few cents.
>
> Calling his disciples to him, Jesus said, "Truly I tell you, this poor widow has put more into the treasury than all the others." (Mk 12:41-43)

As government officials, scribes were well-versed in the law and issues of local governance. Need a marriage certificate? Divorce papers? Loan documents? A mortgage contract? Just go to one of these supercilious scribes, and for a small fee, they will sort it out for you.

In first-century Palestine, every village had at least one scribe, but the system was as corrupt as Vladimir Putin's inner circle. Jesus knew that they had a bit of a scam going, so he accuses them of devouring widows' houses. Jesus was speaking in the tradition of the prophets. Imagine this scenario: a poor woman, who is illiterate and desperate, has just lost her husband, who has not left a will, and she's forced to go to the local scribe to sort out her inheritance. The scribe perceives her vulnerable state and swindles her out of what is rightfully hers. In this way, he "devours" the poor widow's house by cheating her out of her inheritance.

Obviously, this kind of corruption made Jesus furious, and exploitation should incense us too! Perhaps this is why he promises that these scribes will be punished severely for their hypocrisy and corruption (see Mk 12:40 above) and then later refers to them each of them as a "child of hell" (Mt 23:15).

I imagine Jesus sitting there, all riled up about their hypocrisy, their long religious prayers, their expensive clothing, and the way they are cheating widows out of their homes. Then at that precise moment, an actual widow comes along—one of the victims of their schemes—and she gives her last two pennies to the corrupt temple system! What a mess! No wonder Jesus declares that the whole dirty, rotten temple would be torn down (Mk 13:2). This prophecy was fulfilled about forty years later.

These passages reveal how God not only deals with corrupt individuals (Mk 12:40) but also promises that justice will one day come to the entire broken system (Mk 13:2). Jesus' pursuit of justice threatens their political and religious power, causing the various groups of power brokers to set aside their differences and come together to take down their common enemy: this radical and subversive upstart, who is undermining their lucrative side hustles.

In the crucifixion showdown, Caiaphas, the official head honcho of the politically powerful Sadducees, engineers charges against Jesus so that he can be executed by the state as a criminal and insurrectionist. But Jesus forgives his accusers, overcomes sin and death, and triumphs over the forces of darkness that sought to bring him down.

This story reveals how Jesus followed in the tradition of the ancient prophets by calling out corruption and injustice throughout his ministry. This wasn't some side issue, for justice and good news for the poor are at the center of God's kingdom, where people boldly hold their leaders to account because it is right and good for the downtrodden. In this kingdom, Jesus promises that leaders who oppress the poor or hold onto their power through corruption and violence will be held accountable.

JESUS, THE PROPHETIC STORYTELLER

Jesus often spoke out against injustice through storytelling. Though he never wrote a single book on theology, he taught theology wherever he went by telling stories that are still recounted and enjoyed today.

Listening to stories is a universally beloved experience that touches our emotions in a way that cold facts can't. Every major religion uses stories to communicate wisdom and to seek new followers. In a cross-cultural context, stories are still the most effective form of communication. No matter where you go in the world, people love to tell and listen to a good story.

In the Alongsiders movement, we have adopted a narrative approach by combining stories with beautiful artwork created by local artists, which we turn into a monthly comic book that the Alongsiders read with their "little brother" or "little sister." In countries where books are rare, those comic books are as precious as gold.

As the movement has expanded across Asia and into Africa, we have begun working with local artists in Cambodia, India, Pakistan, Indonesia, and Rwanda to create contextualized stories along with locally illustrated comics. We now work in more than twenty-five languages, with hundreds of different versions of the Alongsiders comic book curriculum, which has all been created by local storytellers and artists.

Books and movies also convey stories, and George Orwell's insightful allegory, *Animal Farm*, often resonates like a gong in places of oppression and corruption. After the Alongsiders comic book team started making animated videos so we could offer our training through mobile phones, our media team leader, Lakhina, hatched a plot to translate the 1954 animated *Animal Farm* movie into Khmer, using subtitles.

The translation took a long time, and political tensions were running high, with many arrests for simple Facebook posts, so I was extremely cautious about uploading this video to YouTube. But Lakhina, who was proud of her hard work, uploaded the translation onto her personal account. She didn't mention it to me for several months, but when she showed it to me, I was hesitant—though I promised we could show it publicly someday.

We finally decided to project the movie on an outside wall at Shalom Valley, where construction was beginning to kick into high gear. So Phearom and I invited Mony and our little band of justice-seekers for an overnight retreat. We felt much more comfortable with conducting these "political" discussions face to face because they would be offline and therefore more hidden from government scrutiny.

Unfortunately, the same weekend we planned our movie night, an exiled opposition leader threatened to return to the country, and the cops were all making sure that there were plenty of bullets in their 9mm Soviet pistols. As we made our way down to Shalom Valley in the bus, we saw countless police and soldiers lining the roads, stopping cars, opening trunks, and checking vehicles for anything suspicious. We figured we didn't have anything overtly subversive on us, and we were all so excited to be getting out of the city that we broke out in song as we drove past these troops.

Later that evening, we lay around on pillows strewn across the concrete pad underneath several strands of fairy lights, eating crunchy Khmer snacks as we eagerly waited for the movie to begin. It had been a while since I had seen *Animal Farm*, but after five minutes, I started to get nervous as I realized that the film was much more revolutionary than I had remembered. As the pigs and chickens started waving pitchforks and screaming about taking over the Jones Farm by force, and Farmer Jones began to run for his life, I started to sweat. This movie was about as subtle as a sledgehammer! But we were in the middle of nowhere, I told myself, so there was nothing to worry about.

About fifteen minutes into the movie, Marea, one of the senior leaders of Shalom Valley, sidled up to me and whispered, "The police are here." I sat upright and looked at the entrance of Shalom Valley, where three armed police officers in uniform stood in clear sight of the movie. Marea said that they had come to make sure that we were not engaged in any kind of "political activity."

Meanwhile, the animated sheep and pigs projected on the wall were bleating loudly about revolution and overthrowing the authoritarian regime that was oppressing them. Luckily, they were bleating in English, and I was fairly certain that the police could not see the Khmer subtitles at the bottom of the screen from where they were standing. I gulped and wiped sweat from my forehead.

"Tell them we're watching an animated children's movie," I told Marea, and then I moved to get up. "Look, I'll talk to them."

She placed a hand on my forearm. "No, you stay here. It's better if they don't see any foreigners." She was right—no white savior was needed at this moment of crisis. If I wanted to be an ally, I needed to stay in the background at this crucial juncture. Most prophetic personalities are prone to speak up, but as allies we need to practice great self-discipline. Though everything within me rebelled against letting a twenty-something, mild-mannered, young Cambodian woman deal with three surly, jackbooted, armed police, who looked like the Khmer version of the Nazi infantry, I suppressed my instincts and let her take charge.

The movie continued, but I was no longer watching. As Marea engaged the police, I chewed my fingernails and started to pray. I knew my presence would raise further suspicions and get everyone in more trouble, so I sat back and tried to relax, though I had to fight the urge to get up and try to talk with the police, who ended up staying through the whole two-hour screening of *Animal Farm*, just inches out of sight of the subtitles.

For those two nail-biting hours, Marea, an absolute legend of courage, engaged them in conversation and satisfied them that we weren't causing any trouble. Meanwhile, the rest of us nervously watched Orwell's brilliant insights into authoritarian regimes while the police remained oblivious of its truly subversive nature.

I've since come to the conclusion that the very best storytelling moments occur when there is something real at stake—your freedom, your ideology, the things upon which you've built your life. In a world where safety and comfort have become our idols, we need to tell more dangerous, subversive, and provocative stories. The stories Jesus told eventually got him killed, so as followers of Jesus, why should we expect things to be different for us?

After the police left, we soberly debriefed the movie. The young Cambodians could not believe that in 1954 George Orwell had somehow imagined what would befall their nation in 1975. They were fascinated by the way that the oppressed, once they finally thought they had achieved liberation, had become oppressors themselves. We talked about how we need to find our true freedom in Jesus, or we will repeat the same patterns as those who have gone before us, from one generation to the next.

"Here's the thing, Craig," a young woman said, poking the air to make her point. "That movie doesn't just relate to our lives under the Khmer Rouge. That story describes our lives perfectly today."

Prophetic Lament

Later that weekend, we discussed the upcoming election. The governing regime had imprisoned most of the opposition party leaders, and others had fled into exile. Facebook posts were being monitored, and those who spoke out against human rights abuses were being imprisoned or targeted.

Mony told me that he was now on a blacklist and being watched by government informers. "Be careful, Craig," he warned. "There are even Christian leaders who are currying favor with the government by informing on their fellow believers."

One of our Khmer team members told us that the government was employing people to trawl through social media posts for any antigovernment messages. There was a general sense of paranoia in those weeks before the elections.

Some people began to say online that they wouldn't vote because there was no legitimate opposition party. The government put pressure on local village leaders to force people to vote, making it an act of sedition to refuse to vote. This last bastion of resistance tumbled down quickly. Cambodians had known too much suffering, and most had little stomach for any act of protest.

Mony and our small Bible study group began to grapple with how to respond in this atmosphere of oppression. Protest would be a fast track to jail, but perhaps there was something else we could do? I asked our group how Cambodians expressed their deepest feelings of lament. This conversation opened space for us all to grieve the loss of freedom, integrity, and justice in Cambodia. Then Mony explained that the deepest cultural expression of lament in Cambodia would be to shave one's head and wear all white. "That's what we do when our mother or father dies."

As we looked at each other around the table, an idea began to form. What if we were to lament, truly grieve, for what was happening in this nation by shaving our heads and dressing in white on election day? No one could fault us for a simple act of cultural expression, and yet we would be letting out the deepest groans of our hearts in the ancient biblical tradition. After all, a third of the Psalms are psalms of lament.

We discussed whether it would be possible to gather together in an act of public lament on election day and agreed that it would be too dangerous. "But *you* should do it," they said, turning to me. "We would be immediately arrested and thrown in prison, but as a white foreigner, you could probably get away with something. You should do this at Democracy Square, Craig."

I gulped and wondered what that might look like to be an ally in this way. Not a protest but an act of lament. I imagined myself going to Democracy Square by myself in a low-key ritual of grief on election day. Would I dare? If I were arrested, would they shut down the work of Alongsiders and curtail the efforts of youth who were walking alongside children all over the country?

I prayed and weighed the challenge from my Khmer brothers and sisters to step out in solidarity, even with this tiny act. Ultimately, it seemed like the right thing to do, so I joined our group of Cambodian leaders as we shaved our heads in preparation for the election. Then I would go to Democracy Square alone as they had requested.

Our tiny WhatsApp group became livelier as we shared selfies from a local barbershop, pictures of our beautiful locks falling to the ground, victims of a rusty razor. We ribbed one guy, who was already bald, with jokes about leading the way and "easy sacrifice."

But then Mony got a message that a wider group of people had been forwarding our pictures in WhatsApp. Attached to the message was a photo of me, taken the day before, at the barbershop. The accompanying message read, "Look at this foreigner shaving his hair as a protest in the traditional Khmer way!"

Mony wrote back to the person who had passed it on and asked, "Where did you get this?" The friend who had passed the image to Mony said that the photo had been shown the day before at a government meeting about dissidents and people who were causing political trouble. I was the only foreigner included on their list, and Mony's contact thought it was fascinating to see my creative protest.

We started freaking out about how government spies had gotten hold of my photo. I had only shared it with our own small group on WhatsApp. Was there an informer? We didn't think so, but the election was the next day, and we were pretty sure the government knew I was planning to go to Democracy Square. A coworker pointed out that for several days someone was parked for long hours in front of our office, keeping an eye on us. I started getting worried that I was about to be arrested simply for being an ally.

Becoming an Ally

What had started as a lighthearted conversation among friends around a table had suddenly become risky. As my fear and anxiety mounted, I worried about what might happen to the Alongsiders ministry and Shalom Valley. Would I get my friends and family in trouble? What was my role as an outsider? As I grappled with my place as an outsider, who had suddenly found myself swept up in a very tense and dangerous unjust situation, I jotted down the following guidelines for those who are seeking to become (outsider) allies instead of (insider) prophets.

First, start with self-awareness. Recognize that you are a person of privilege, who has a certain amount of protection simply because of your passport. Soberly consider the dangers you are facing and then consider the dangers that local prophets face. Most likely, these dangers will not be the same. Weigh the costs together with local activists and allow them to make their own decisions about how much danger they are willing to face. You may be gung-ho because you are untouchable. Don't judge locals if they are more reticent; their families, livelihoods, and even their very lives may be on the line.

Second, educate yourself on the issues. Acting out of ignorance or untamed passion is not helpful. Take the time to listen deeply to those affected and consider your own complicity in the injustice that they face. What role did your nation, or people who look like you, play in the history of this unjust situation? As a citizen of a country that may have played a part in oppressing the people of this nation, what responsibility do you have to speak out about this injustice?

Third, use your freedom and circles of influence. As an English-speaking outsider with access to Western media and contacts, you bring something very helpful to the table: the potential to get the word out. International attention can often help (or sometimes hinder) a local cause. You may be able to pick up a phone or send an email that a local leader cannot. Use this liberty for the good of those who are being oppressed.

Fourth, amplify the voices of local activists. Sometimes, being a voice for the voiceless is just another excuse to place ourselves at the center of someone else's story. This impulse can become a subtle way of becoming a false savior, pushing ourselves to the forefront and taking the place of honor (Lk 14:8). When we draw attention to ourselves, we marginalize the poor all over again. When we attempt to be a voice for the voiceless, we fail to recognize that they already have a voice. When we speak for people who may prefer to speak for themselves, we reinforce their voicelessness. We confuse not being heard with having nothing to say.

When we look at Jesus, he often encourages people to use their voices. He asks beggars and people with leprosy what they want him to do, though it must have seemed obvious if the guy he was talking to was blind or covered in sores. Arundhati Roy, an Indian activist and thinker, once said, "There's really no such thing as the 'voiceless.' There are only the deliberately silenced, or the preferably unheard."[16]

Finally, count the cost. Any outsider ally who comes alongside insider prophets must grapple with Jesus' call to take up our cross and sacrifice for those whom we serve. Because we come with power, we may not be called to sacrifice as much. While I might be in danger of being deported, which is traumatic, my Khmer friends might end up floating face down in the Mekong River. Whatever the cost, we must count it.

77

Prophetic Solidarity

When election day dawned, I woke up early after a restless night. I picked up the white shirt and trousers that had been made especially for the day and got dressed. I pinned a black piece of cloth to my chest as a final touch, a symbol of grieving and lament in Khmer culture. Then I got on my motorbike and began the long drive across town to Democracy Square.

Nay and my children had gone to Australia for the school holidays, urged by friends and family to leave the country during these times of political turmoil. No one would be alerted if I was arrested, but I knew that word would still get out fairly quickly.

When Democracy Square was less than a mile away, I knew I was reaching the point of no return. If there were soldiers waiting for me at Democracy Square, it would be hard to escape. After all, I was a tall, white foreigner with a shaved head, dressed in traditional white funeral clothes.

I slowed my motorbike to a crawl and considered turning around. Was making such a feeble statement for justice worth all this danger? Did I dare to be an ally in the way I'd been asked to?

In the end, I sensed God's peace and continued on my way. I knew that the Alongsiders movement was a grassroots movement and was not reliant on me. With so little structure and paid staff, there was not much the government could easily shut down.

I also sensed that the greatest gift I could give my Cambodian friends was to be a wise and bold friend, carrying out small acts of courage that might encourage and embolden others. I knew that the Alongsiders themselves carried out similar small acts of courage every day as they sought to reach beyond their comfort zones. I revved the accelerator and turned the corner to Democracy Square, fully prepared for this to be my final act of freedom in Cambodia before I was jailed or deported.

5

DANGER #2
COMPLICITY

The dominant religion on the planet is not Christianity, Islam, Hinduism, or Judaism, but the pervasive faith in violence.

WALTER WINK

WHEN I ARRIVED AT DEMOCRACY SQUARE, it was mostly empty, desolate, and eerie. Instead of finding soldiers waiting to arrest me, I saw a homeless woman sleeping on a raised concrete slab in a shady corner. Nearby, her young son kicked around an empty can.

I breathed a sigh of relief and kicked down the stand on my motorbike. Then I walked over and plunked myself down under a solitary tree that was sprouting from the middle of the concrete, a sign of life and a place of shade, though it was still early in the morning. Opening my Bible, I tried to read and pray, but it was hard to concentrate. My anxiety was still running high, so I wandered over to the woman, who had awakened and was squatting in the shade, resting her head on her crossed arms, groaning softly.

I squatted down beside her and offered the traditional Khmer greeting, pressing my hands together beneath my chin, and addressing her as "Ming," which means "aunty-who-is-younger-than-my-parents," as a gesture of respect. Her yellow eyes and skeletal frame were a dead giveaway for alcoholism and serious liver disease. I'd looked into similar eyes in the addicts I'd met in the Downtown Eastside of Vancouver and the alcoholics who scraped by in the slums of Phnom Penh—eyes that reflected the pain and sorrow of a broken world.

She began to whisper hoarsely, and I leaned forward to listen as the story of her life tumbled out. As she spoke about the Khmer Rouge years, her eyes filled with tears that spilled down her weathered and sunburned cheeks. Like so many traumatized Cambodians, she had self-medicated with cheap alcohol to survive her long, hard days and bury the memories. Who could blame her?

Her boy came closer and shyly tugged on my white shirttail. Shifting to look at him, I patted his shoulder and smiled. I had already lived through three post-cancer years, and I knew that God was giving me ample opportunities to fulfill my promise to care for the fatherless in small ways.

But I wanted to do more than pat this boy on the shoulder. I wanted to address the root causes of his situation. As Bonhoeffer said, "We are not to simply bandage the wounds of victims beneath the wheels of injustice, we are to drive a spoke into the wheel itself."[1] I reminded myself that laying down our lives doesn't usually happen in a blaze of glory, but in tiny moments as we face myriad choices every day—tiny moments of faithfulness and sacrifice.

Since my plan had been to fast and pray in the square, I hadn't brought along any food that I could share, so I jumped on my bike and rode to the nearest market to pick up something nutritious for this mother and her young son. When I got back, they hungrily shared the container of rice and pork that I offered to them.

I thought about the millions of others who were eking out an existence in abandoned spaces across Cambodia (let alone the world), traumatized by war and violence, the victims of political maneuvering, living from the scraps that tumbled from the tables of the elite. I thought of the next generation, their beautiful children, who were growing up in a country that was no longer at war but not really any better for those at the bottom of the heap. As I returned to my shade tree, I thought that if God had asked me to spend the day in prayer and lament, perhaps I was meant not only to grieve the actions of the Cambodian government but to examine what I might have to lament as a descendant of people that had engaged in ongoing colonialism and warfare around the world.

I am a dual citizen of Canada and New Zealand, with ancestral roots in England. Was I somehow complicit in the misfortune that had befallen this woman and her son? When we relocate to nations with histories of colonialism, war, and exploitation, we are often blind to our own complicated national identity. This is true not only for people of European descent but also for those of Chinese, Japanese, Korean, and other ethnicities. We all have our complicated historical atrocities. This is not just about white people.

It struck me that people living in the wealthy and "developed" countries of the world often referred to nations such as Cambodia as "developing countries," but a more honest and humble acknowledgment would recognize them as countries who are struggling to recover from being ruthlessly exploited and colonized.[2]

Our forefathers may have directly or indirectly oppressed the forefathers of our new neighbors. Even if our own biological ancestors weren't directly involved, the tone of our skin or the shape of our faces may remind local people of those who carried out historical injustices against them. After all, most Cambodians never really differentiated between me and an American or a European. For the most part, they called us all *Barang* (French), the ethnicity of their colonizers. In Khmer eyes, every white person is a colonizer. One of the most dangerous sins that an outsider ally can bring into a situation of injustice is the failure to recognize our complicity in the shared history of our peoples.

SUBVERSIVE PRAYING

As I sat in Democracy Square on election day, I reflected on the book of Daniel, which our Alongsiders team had been studying for the previous few months. Daniel 9 in particular had been shaking my Western worldview in some deeply uncomfortable ways.[3]

First, I was struck by how Daniel was so dedicated to God that he nearly became a lion's chew toy because of his prayer routine. Sometimes faithfulness is provocative. Second, his prayers were not personal, individualistic, "Bless-me-and-my-family" prayers as I was taught to pray in Sunday school. Instead, he started by acknowledging that he was living within a certain political milieu: "the first year of Darius son of Xerxes" (Dan 9:1).

If Daniel were living today, he would acknowledge that he was living in the first term of a certain prime minister or the lame-duck year of a certain president. His prayer was rooted in an awareness of the political context of his times. As the old saying goes, we should pray with a newspaper in one hand and a Bible in the other—reading both the Word and the world at all times.

Third, Daniel knelt in repentance. Though Daniel was pretty much blameless personally, he still prayed in the following way:

> We have sinned and done wrong. We have been wicked and have rebelled; we have turned away from your commands and laws. . . .
>
> We and our kings, our princes and our ancestors are covered with shame, LORD, because we have sinned against you. . . . All Israel has transgressed your law and turned away, refusing to obey you. (Dan 9:5, 8-11)

Daniel was certainly not personally responsible for Israel's waywardness. He didn't chisel wooden idols, eat a bacon sandwich, or run around causing chaos with prostitutes. Daniel was a good guy, a missionary serving in a foreign land. He was blameless and righteous. Yet here he was, confessing and repenting for the sins of his people—not just his currently alive-and-kicking people but also his dead-and-buried people, his ancestors. Now that is one wide-ranging prayer of repentance! God responded favorably to Daniel (whose name literally means "God is my judge") by giving him a vision of how God was going to discipline and restore the nation of Israel.

The Bible is filled with Israel's story—the good, the bad, and the brutally ugly. They were faithful in preserving this story in order to teach their children to repent. If I were recording my nation's history, I'd be tempted to record only the triumphs and victories. I'd be tempted to leave out all our failures and mistakes—thus perpetuating the myth that we have no need to repent. But Israel didn't give in to this temptation, and thank God—that truthful history forms part of our sacred Scriptures today.

As a white Westerner, I have been steeped in a very personalized worldview. As a child in church, I was taught that I was responsible to repent only for my sins, not anyone else's. I was taught that I was responsible only for my choices, not my ancestors'—and I certainly didn't have to answer for the actions of my government. Those things were completely outside the scope of my concern. Yet many other cultures (including Cambodia) teach a more holistic worldview, in which we are all tied together, making us complicit in the sins of our people. Though it runs against Western individualism, this is the worldview that the Bible affirms.

My own great-great-granddaddies lived in Sussex, England, a place once colonized by the Romans. They then eventually became part of the original influx of Brits into New Zealand. They made a treaty with the indigenous Māori population of the country that outlined a kind of "Bill of Rights" for both Māori and Pākehā (those of European ancestry), establishing a local identity and invitation to share the land together.[4]

I am grateful for this historical covenant of hospitality and my resulting identity as a Pākehā New Zealander with roots in Sussex, England. Ethnically, white is not so much a race as a club designed to keep other people out. Before we were white, we were Irish, British, Scottish, and German—and sometime later, the Italians got added to the "white club."[5]

Sadly, the European settlers—those who had been welcomed as Pākehā—broke that treaty time and time again. They stole land from the Māori inhabitants. They trampled the Māori culture and sought to snuff it out. They killed indigenous people in the stampede for wealth. All of this was horribly wrong.

While I didn't do any of these things personally, according to Daniel, because my ancestors did, repentance and reparation are appropriate responses for me. This dynamic is often overlooked by those who work cross-culturally. Every ally, indeed every outsider, must grapple with its implications.

Though we didn't personally colonize the people of a struggling country, our forerunners may have. Though we didn't personally put chains on their ankles, our ancestors may have. Though we didn't personally drop bombs from B-52 planes on their traumatized children, our nation may have. Moreover, we have often personally benefited from the actions of our ancestors. Another word for this historical benefit or upper hand is *privilege*.

We often want to remain blind to our own complicity, but, with blind Bartimaeus, we can cry out again and again for Jesus to have mercy on us (Mk 10:46-48). Rather than sitting on the side of the road feeling despondent and apathetic as we are silenced by stern onlookers who keep telling us to be quiet, we can take courage, jump up, run to Jesus, and ask him to open our eyes so we will be able to see (Mk 10:46, 48-51).

As I sat under that little shade tree in Democracy Square, reflecting on Daniel's prayer and Bartimaeus's cries for mercy, I sensed Jesus asking me the same question he had asked Bartimaeus: "What do you want me to do for you?" (Mk 10:51). Humbling myself, I asked Jesus to open my eyes so that I could become more deeply aware of the political and historical context of Cambodia; then I began to pray and repent for the sins of my people.

Though I wasn't arrested that day and my act of lament most likely went unnoticed, an empty square dedicated to the political process turned out to be the place where Jesus invited me to come face to face with the brokenness of the world and to mourn and repent for my own part in it.

RESTORING OUR BROKEN WORLD

Our Shalom Valley leadership team continued to feel stirred to respond to the deeper needs of vulnerable children by establishing an adventure camp as a center for healing and training in the way of peace, but we still did not know how we would pay for the land or the construction. Then, a few months after Phearom first found the parcel of land, I returned to Vancouver for a visit, and a four-year-old girl from our Downtown Eastside neighborhood handed me a sweetly decorated envelope stuffed with her pocket money. "This is for little kids to go to camp," she whispered. I lifted the envelope with both hands to the sky and silently asked God to multiply it as he had the loaves and fishes.

Another early donation came from a poor Cambodian church that was excited about the vision. They had passed around an offering bag and come up with a surprising amount. Their generosity reminded me that we should never assume that the poor can't contribute. Jesus didn't exclude them—and neither should we!

Then Nay connected with a Cambodian Christian woman in Kep, who donated from her landscaping company trees and supplies worth thousands of dollars. Remarkably, bit by bit (and often just in time for a deadline), the rest of the funds began to trickle in—primarily from within Asia but also from partners around the world.[6]

As we began to build the camp, the Shalom Valley team continued to grow. My sixty-five-year-old father worked regularly at the land, swinging a pickaxe alongside Pon, a Cambodian Christian whom my dad had met while Pon was driving a *tuk-tuk*[7] around Kep. Pon was very well connected, so he became our local informant and fixer. He was well liked by everyone.

Sreypon, who lived in Kep, joined us after her pastor introduced her to us. She'd been praying for God to give her a good job with Christians, and as soon as she arrived, she started chopping at weeds in the hot sun alongside Pon and my dad.

A lanky, bespectacled Dutchman named Mart-Jan came on board as a volunteer engineer. He provided technical oversight for what turned out to be a major construction project. Mart-Jan developed highly detailed plans, made technical calculations, and was committed to a level of workmanship that would ensure the project would be built to last for decades rather than just a few years. When a Singaporean architectural firm offered to do the technical drawings pro bono, we knew the project would come together.

As we continued to clear the land, we uncovered a large round crater that was about the size and shape of a spa pool. Pon identified it as a bomb crater. "These are all over the place in this area, from the American bombing," he told us.

The name Shalom Valley made more and more sense as we continued to learn how this piece of land had been scarred by war. The valley had once provided refuge to those who were fleeing violence, and we hoped it would provide refuge once again. After we found the bomb crater, we invited friends and leaders from around the country to a groundbreaking ceremony, where we hiked around, sweating and praying solemnly at little prayer stations we had set up all over the land, each with a different shalom passage from the Bible.

RECOVERING A BIBLICAL VISION OF SHALOM

We included Jeremiah 29:11 in one of these prayer stations: "'For I know the plans I have for you,' declares the LORD, 'plans to prosper you and not to harm you, plans to give you hope and a future.'"

While this verse is well known, it is probably one of the most misunderstood and misapplied verses in all of Scripture. The word *shalom* here has been translated as "prosper"—obscuring the meaning in English. Shalom is not just a Jewish greeting, and it goes much deeper and further than having a few extra bucks in your pocket. Yet many people wrongly understand the word *shalom* to be economic prosperity, as if this were a personal promise to fold up and pop in our back pocket, something to pull out whenever we need a little boost from our vending-machine God. No matter what the prosperity preachers say, shalom is not merely about economic prosperity, nor even the absence of war. Rather, shalom is a big, beautiful vision embodying all that God desires for the whole creation. God wants to restore *all* things. Shalom is God's answer to the question, What *should* the world be like?

Osheta Moore describes shalom as "God's dream for the world as it should be: nothing broken, nothing missing, everything made whole."[8] That is, God desires for us to live in harmony with each other. In short, shalom is the Hebrew way of describing God's kingdom on earth as it is in heaven.

While Jeremiah 29:11 makes a beautiful, radical, earth-shattering promise to an entire nation, this promise hinges on God's command to the people of Israel in Jeremiah 29:7: "Seek the peace and prosperity [*shalom*] of the city to which I have carried you into exile." This command conveys God's deep longing for his people to discover how he sees the whole world by pursuing the well-being of their whole community.

In God's beautiful picture of this city of shalom, God describes sustainable building, planting, and caring for the whole creation so that everyone will have good nutrition and good relationships with family and others, doing business in a just way, ignoring false spiritual teachings, and even having babies (Jer 29:5-6). Shalom is the full picture of life in abundance, of living in community together.

Though Christians often claim to have a vision for society, we have gained a reputation for an extremely narrow political agenda. If you ask the average nonbeliever in North America today what Christians stand for, they will likely say, "Not for, but against." Christians stand against gay marriage and abortion.

Sadly, we are not well known for seeking the shalom—or well-being—of our entire community. Rather than pushing our pet issues and being known for what we fight against, we need to earn the right to be heard by clearly demonstrating over a sustained period of time that we are seeking the good of the whole community—not just our own good. This even includes seeking the good of those with whom we might disagree because Jesus calls us to love *all* our neighbors.[9]

While Western Christians will spill onto the streets with protest signs and Chick-fil-A take-out bags if any government limitations are placed on our freedom to worship, how do we respond when other religious groups experience persecution? Are we just as quick to come to their defense? When Buddhists, Muslims, or Jedi Knights are not allowed to build a place of worship or gather together, do we speak out in their defense? Do we "do to others what [we] would have them do to [us]" (Mt 7:12)?

When members of the gay and transgender communities are denied access to housing, bathrooms, or other basic services, do we wish homelessness, hunger, or soiled pants on them? Or do we sign petitions and march in defense of our fellow human beings so they will be allowed to meet their basic human needs? Do we love them as our brothers and sisters? After all, we're called to love everyone—our neighbors, our enemies, and every person in between—even if we do not agree with them.

When refugees are denied assistance, caged, or refused safe harbor, do we speak out and protest in their defense as if they were our own children? Or do we prioritize the people of our own nation and tribe over the children of our neighbors? Would Jesus refer to a mother and child who walk a thousand miles to flee violence as illegals? Would he call those who cross wild oceans to bring their children to safety aliens? Or would he honor these parents as heroes? As followers of Jesus and the God of the Bible, we are called to recognize that every single human being is made in the image of God (Gen 1:27).

Perhaps it's worth reflecting on these questions before we travel overseas. If we can't figure out how to love and respect people of other religions and practices in our own passport country, where they are a powerless minority, how can we hope to love them in other countries, where they are the majority? If we aren't prepared to love across all divides, we will pack our suitcases full of toxic antagonism before we ever board the plane.

Honestly, I've struggled all my life to love my enemies. My heart is so very hard. If this is making you uncomfortable, don't give up. Join me on the journey. We can struggle together.

LOVING ACROSS BORDERS

While some say, "Love your nation," Jesus says, "Love your neighbor." Love for a nation is limited by borders and tribes, but love for our neighbors transcends borders and tribes—and has the power to transform the whole world.

When we say we want to follow Jesus, we are called to pledge our allegiance to Jesus alone, which means we pledge to live a life of selflessness rather than selfishness. Jesus preached the principle of shalom from the side of a mountain: "I tell you, love your enemies and pray for those who persecute you" (Mt 5:44). Paul summarized the whole of the Old Testament law in a single verse from Leviticus: "Love your neighbor as yourself" (Gal 5:14; Lev 19:18). If Christians around the world actually lived out this vision of love in their homes, workplaces, and neighborhoods, it would revolutionize our politics, faith, communities, and countries—indeed, every nation of the world!

When we speak out only for ourselves, we will be seen as yet another lobby group and will never earn the right to be heard. But when we begin to speak out for others, we will be known for our goodwill, and we will earn a reputation for speaking out for everybody.

If we want to influence our communities—and the whole world—with the love of Christ, we need to give up our tunnel vision and abandon our single-issue voting. We have to take a wiser, more nuanced approach to political engagement. This isn't about voting left or right—left and right are just wings on the same old partisan bird. This is about devoting the whole of our lives—how we vote, how we talk, how we live, how we love—to the shalom priorities of Jesus.

This commitment to shalom calls us to work consistently to preserve all life. This includes unborn children, and it also includes caring for all children after they are born—especially those who are born into poverty. Working consistently to preserve all life includes protecting those who are condemned to death in our criminal justice systems. Working consistently to preserve all life also includes caring for the entire creation since it is the source of life for everything on earth.

When Christians speak out against military overreach, the left applauds. When Christians speak out against abortion, the right applauds. When Christians lovingly and consistently work together to preserve all life, the boundaries that separate the left from the right begin to fade, and the world will be able to see God's shalom healing and restoring the whole world.

My friend Shane Claiborne, an activist who is known for writing books and wearing weird clothes that he sewed himself, is a holy troublemaker for Christ. He has dedicated his life to overcoming the death penalty in the United States. In his writings, he reveals how the modern death penalty has succeeded in America—not in spite of Christians but because of Christians.[10] How far have we strayed from the nonviolent, consistently life-preserving, shalom teachings of Jesus?

The pursuit of shalom—seeking first God's kingdom on earth as it is in heaven—must extend beyond our national borders and include the lives of our nation's enemies and their children (Mt 6:33). How can we bomb another country, such as

Cambodia, and say that we are seeking God's shalom by promoting their well-being? Once we know Jesus and catch his shalom vision, how can we take up deadly arms against another human being ever again?

This is not some obscure, newly discovered pacifist stance held by a few radicals and crazy hippies. The earliest Christians—who prayerfully chose the canon of Scripture, debated the creeds, and built the first churches—overwhelmingly condemned the practice of killing our enemies. The early church held this pacifist stance until the conversion of Emperor Constantine in AD 313. All major Christian theologians resolutely refused to pick up a weapon and slay another human being until this time, when Christianity gained political power. Once the political power was on our side, Christians suddenly became willing to wield it against others.

Origen, one of the most influential figures in early Christian theology, stated categorically that "we no longer take sword against a nation, nor do we learn any more to make war, having become sons of peace for the sake of Jesus."[11] Origen is echoing the simple command of Jesus that we are to love our enemies and pray for those who persecute us (Mt 5:44). We cannot love our enemies while shooting or bombing them.

The litmus test for our love of God is whether we love our neighbors.[12] And the litmus test for our love of neighbors is whether we love our enemies. If we say we love God, love our neighbors, and love our enemies, we will reject killing them, which is a slap in the face of a life-preserving God.

NURTURING SHALOM IN THE VALLEY

During our groundbreaking ceremony at Shalom Valley, as we made our way under the blazing sun from one prayer station to another across the war-scarred land on that hidden hillside, I reflected on various aspects of God's amazing vision of shalom. At each station, I prayerfully invited God to help me become more and more of an ally, to become someone who would pursue God's vision of shalom with passion and humility as I repented of the violence in my own heart and history.

When we arrived at the bomb crater, we reflected on Jesus, whom Isaiah refers to as the "Prince of Peace," the *Sar* Shalom (Is 9:6). Jesus, our Messiah, laid down his life so that the whole world might receive healing and live in shalom:

> But he was pierced for our transgressions,
>   he was crushed for our iniquities;
> the punishment that brought us peace [*shalom*] was on him,
>   and by his wounds we are healed. (Is 53:5)

As we lingered together by the bomb crater, thanking God for that potent symbol of new life and hope emerging out of a place of death and destruction, a vision began to form among us about how this site could spark Cambodians' imagination for God's shalom in their country. We knew there was a desperate need for young Cambodians to know the history of their land, and we prayed that God would help them find healing and reconciliation amid the ashes. We were moving from violence to shalom in the footsteps of Jesus, the Prince of Peace.

6

FROM EVANGELIST (INSIDER) TO SEEKER (OUTSIDER)

We do not go to mission lands to bring Jesus Christ,
as much as to uncover him where he already is.

CATHERINE DOHERTY

ONE AFTERNOON SHORTLY AFTER our groundbreaking ceremony, I got an urgent phone call from my dad at the Shalom Valley building site. "The bulldozers are working their way toward the bomb crater, and it'll be gone by the end of the day," he warned. Half a dozen frantic phone calls later, we managed to save the bomb crater from the bulldozers by having the dormitory building shifted about twelve meters to the left.

Though a few feathers were ruffled, we knew it was important to preserve the bomb crater because scars are a potent symbol of healing, emblems of old pain. They do not need to be hidden away, covered up, or filled with dirt. Instead, they need to be displayed as life lessons, badges of honor, markers of victory over death. When we are still standing, breathing, and walking around with old scars, our very lives communicate that those wounds don't define us—and won't have the final say.

I was a walking testament to this bomb-crater theology myself. The scars from my many cancer surgeries plotted a visible map of that painful season across my lower belly. Though those scars have long since healed, they continue to serve as a beautiful reminder of what I have overcome.

To memorialize the bomb crater as a potent symbol of the life that can emerge after death, Pon and his team hauled bags of trash and rubble out of the crater and planted grass inside. They also planted a low "hedge of protection" at the top and laid a red stone pathway around its edge. As we tended to the work of beautifying the crater, the dormitory building slowly rose up beside it.

Once the grass was growing and the pathway was finished, we started hosting more groups at Shalom Valley for camps and retreats. One group was composed mostly of young Khmer leaders, but it included an older man, Pastor Sokha, who had lived through the Khmer Rouge years. As we stood around the edge of the bomb crater, Phearom invited the group to kick off their shoes. The smell of the forest wafted down the mountainside on a gentle breeze, and there was a deep sense of peace as we stood, barefoot, in silence.

Then he asked everyone to step into the bomb crater and find a seat on the grass. A murmur went through the group as everyone tentatively stepped forward and felt the grass between their bare toes. As Pastor Sokha searched for a place to sit, his eyes squinted in recognition, and then he bent down and gently plucked a tiny leaf from a plant that was growing inside the crater. He held the leaf in the air, beaming with pride. "This is one of the herbs that kept us alive during the Khmer Rouge years! We used this to treat our wounds and infections when we had no medicine. This herb saved our lives!"

Phearom and the group of younger Cambodians gathered around Sokha, enthralled, as they examined the plant and peppered him with questions. Once everyone sat down, we reflected on the connections between the bomb crater and Jesus' suffering. "This bomb crater is a scar on this land," I said in Khmer. "It's a symbol of the wounds and scars we all carry with us from the hurt and violence of our lives." I lifted my shirt and showed everyone the cancer scars on my belly. "But we follow One who knew what it was like to be hurt and rejected, who knew the scourge of a whip on his back, who knew the pain of an iron nail being driven through his feet and hands. We follow the scarred One." As I lowered my shirt, several others spoke about how God was still at work in their communities, bringing life from death, just like that life-giving herb sprouting in the bomb crater.

After people shared, we began to imagine the scene when Jesus appeared to his disciples after his death. As they all struggled to believe that death had not had the final word, Jesus joined them at the table, picked up some bread with his scarred hands, blessed it, broke it, and gave it to them with outstretched hands. We talked about how the disciples must have immediately remembered the words Jesus had spoken to them before his death: "This is my body given for you" (Lk 22:19). Then he showed them his wounds and said, "Look at my hands and my feet" (Lk 24:39), inviting them to feel his scars (Jn 20:27). We grew silent as we thought of our own scars and how Jesus had been willing to feel all the vulnerability and pain that we have to face as humans. Breaking the silence, I said, "And then Jesus—who had just been to hell and back—asked his friends for something to eat" (Lk 24:41).

Laughing, I looked up at Phearom, and as our eyes met, I sensed God's resurrection power all around us. Both of us had received the gift of new life amid the contours of death.

Seeker or Evangelist?

If there is one thing missionaries are known for historically, it is evangelism. After all, when Jesus said, "I am the way and the truth and the life" (Jn 14:6), he was inviting us to rearrange our lives around the story of his life—and to extend this beautiful invitation to others. For some, the evangelistic impulse is very straightforward, but when Nay and I returned to Cambodia, we began to wrestle with the ethics and baggage of evangelism by outsiders.

I had recently read about the visit of a famous American preacher to Myanmar (formerly known as Burma)[1]. The preacher wrote about going from hut to hut in a Burmese slum, sharing the gospel through a translator, and he said that the more people he shared the gospel with, the more alive he felt.

But as I reflected on his story, something began to sit uncomfortably within me. You see, I knew this preacher's translator from my previous visits to Myanmar. The translator was also a faithful and gifted Burmese pastor, but the way the story was framed, the foreign evangelist was the hero at the center of the narrative. The story irked me because I knew that the Burmese translator was immeasurably better suited to sharing the gospel in that situation than this new arrival, who didn't even speak the language. I also knew that, in all likelihood, this local translator had already had multiple opportunities to speak with these people in their own heart language and to share the gospel with them himself because this Burmese pastor already had a thriving ministry in that community.

Try to imagine this scenario from the perspective of those community members. An American arrives in your slum community, accompanied by a local minister, whom you already know and respect. The local minister asks if he and this foreigner can enter your home and have a chat. You welcome them with open arms because you have been taught that it is honorable to extend hospitality to strangers, especially if they are wealthier and more powerful than you. Moreover, the visitor is obviously foreign, which might mean that relief supplies could be forthcoming from his wealthy connections back in his home country. As a person living in poverty, you know this power dynamic very well, so you are welcoming and agreeable.

After these visitors come into your home, the American starts to tell you (through the local minister) all about his personal story of life in the United States and what God means to him. He talks a lot about "God" and "love" and "sin." If you are a Buddhist, like 90 percent of the people in Myanmar, you understand that God is everything and nothing. The sun is god.

The moon is god. The king is god. There are many "gods," but you don't know which god this man is talking about.

Even worse, this foreigner tells you that "God loves the world," but as a Buddhist, you find this idea shameful and strange. Love implies attachment, and according to Buddha's Four Noble Truths, attachment to things causes sin. Buddhist religion teaches you to detach—not to attach or love—so that you can escape the cycle of reincarnation and enter nirvana. As a Burmese Buddhist, you think that this "loving god" must be full of unholy passion and therefore must be a sinner.

Hard as you try, you can't get your head around this man's foreign concepts, and though the translator is someone you know and respect, you begin to wonder if he is translating the American correctly. So you listen politely to the confusing description about this god that is a sinner, along with a lot of other things that you don't understand, and then the American visitor asks if you would like to be saved in order to experience God's love.

You can sense that you are supposed to do whatever this foreigner is asking you to do, but you don't understand what being "saved" means. You know that relationships are more important than anything else in your community and that good relationships with people who have power could make the difference between your family's comfort and suffering. So, even though you don't really understand what the man is talking about, you figure you have nothing to lose and everything to gain by saying you would like to be saved. You sense that this is the smart move to make in this odd situation.

Then the American tells you to close your eyes and bow your head and repeat some phrases after him. Afterward, both he and the translator are very excited and happy, and you feel pleased to have had the opportunity to invest in this relationship, which holds even more promise than your relationship with the local minister, as he is poor and doesn't have nearly as much power or prestige. You smile widely and agree to pose for photos with your guests, hoping that the local gossip about your foreign visitor will win you some status in your community.

FISHING IN FOREIGN WATERS

The American preacher in the scenario above later described the situation as follows:

> I feel like I've been fishing in the same pond my whole life and now there's like thousands of other fishermen at the same pond, and our lines are getting tangled and everyone's fighting over stupid things, and one guy tries some new lure and we go, "Oh he caught a fish; let's all try his method!" And it just feels like, what are we all doing here?
>
> What if I heard of a lake that's like a five-mile hike away, and no one's fishing in it. And they're saying, "Man, the fish are biting—just throw a hook in there and they'll go for it!" Man, I'll make that five-mile hike if I love fishing.[2]

While this story has a healthy dose of preacher's hyperbole, it reinforces the perception that there are hardly any local evangelists in Asia, which is a massive continent with wide disparities in terms of numbers of believers from country to country and community to community.

While it may seem as if there is no one "fishing" in the "pond" of the Asian continent, there are actually millions and millions of passionate Christians all through Asia, and many of them are actively sharing the gospel contextually in their own local communities. Tens of thousands even relocate as missionaries to other parts of their own countries. They are far and away the most effective people to reach their neighbors with the gospel because they share a common worldview, culture, and language.

The American preacher in this scenario may not have fully internalized the fact that sharing the gospel in Asia is completely different from sharing Christ in a Judeo-Christian context, where concepts such as God and love have a shared meaning. At this point in history, Asia probably doesn't need more outsiders sharing an unintelligible foreign gospel through translators—especially outsiders who fly in and out and "share" the gospel without living it out in the midst of those whom they are inviting to be "saved." Throughout almost all the world there are competent local ministers who are able to contextualize and share the gospel in meaningful ways that make sense to their own people.

Perhaps we need to rethink the American preacher's fishing story. While the metaphor of fishermen being equipped to catch fish in any pond is rooted in biblical imagery, it doesn't fit the non-Western context for several key reasons. First, the "new pond" actually already has a lot of local fishermen. We just need to train our eyes to see them by recognizing and affirming the role of local evangelists. Second, the local fishermen in that pond are much better equipped to fish there than an outsider. They know the local "bait" because they share a common worldview with their neighbors. Finally, outsiders who try to fish in that pond without understanding the local power dynamics will end up changing the pond's ecosystem in unhelpful—and quite likely detrimental—ways.

So what is the role of an outsider who has a passion and gift for evangelism?

Become a Seeker

Let's look at Paul's posture as he wandered among the Athenians, looking at their statues, seeking to discover how God had already revealed himself in their culture and local religion (Acts 17:22). Like Paul, as outsiders we must come into any new context with a posture of deep humility. We cannot presume that we are "bringing Jesus" to any place because Jesus is already there—even if his name is not yet known. Instead of arriving as experts, we need to come as seekers who are looking for Jesus in the cultural touchpoints, local stories, and everyday lives of the people—even if they are steeped in local religion and culture.

We can see Jesus everywhere if we open our eyes and hearts to seek him—just as our little group found Jesus in the bomb crater that day. Every good and perfect thing comes from God above (Jas 1:17); wherever we see hints of God's goodness—even in the most unlikely places—we can give thanks to him.

This posture of gratitude, grace, humility, and wonder stands in stark contrast to the antagonistic, aggressive, us-versus-them approach of so many foreign evangelists. Seekers need to come into any new context with appreciative inquiry, opening their eyes to discover how God has already revealed himself in the midst of his beloved people. Then they can love the people as God already loves them and offer themselves in service to the work that God is already doing in that place.

▼　　　　　　　THE SEEKER　　　　　　　◢

Seekers come searching for cultural touchpoints as a way of bridging the universal truth of the gospel with local understanding. Seekers are enthusiasts for contextualization, storytelling, and creativity. As outsiders, they come as students of language and culture, and they are more likely to ask questions than offer answers. They work with evangelist-insiders to understand and communicate what the kingdom of God looks like in each new context.

SEEK CULTURAL TOUCHPOINTS

In my own journey of seeking to discover cultural touchpoints in Cambodia, I asked Nay's mother, Yin, how she came to faith in the refugee camp in Thailand, where she was surrounded by foreign missionaries, as well as local believers. Yin told me that her grandmother was deeply immersed in Buddhist practice and the ancient teachings of the Buddha, who lived about five hundred years before Jesus. Yin recalled sitting on her grandmother's knee when she was a young girl, listening to the old religious tales. In a soft voice, her grandmother recounted the story of Preah Sa'a Maitreya, an ancient Khmer Buddhist prophecy. "Yin, this god we are worshiping now is not the one true God. That God is yet to come to us."

She lowered her voice and gathered Yin in her embrace. "Buddha never claimed to be a god. He was a holy and enlightened man. But Buddha said that there will be One who comes after. In the palms of his hands and in the flat of his feet will be the design of a disc, in his side will be a stab wound, and his forehead will have marks like scars. This Holy One will be the golden boat who will carry you over the cycle of rebirths all the way to the highest heaven [Nirvana]."[3]

These stories about Preah Sa'a Maitreya stayed with Yin. As she lived through the Khmer Rouge regime and then escaped to Thailand through the jungle, she tucked these things away in her heart and tried to pray to this one true God. This God, whose name she did not yet know, was already answering her prayers.

When Yin and Nay, along with Nay's younger brother, arrived in the Thai refugee camp, Khao-I-Dang, they were assigned a thatch hut, where they would begin their next season of life. They were grateful for the emergency rations and safe refuge that they found there, but Yin's physical health was poor. After carrying her children through the jungle, miraculously avoiding landmines at every turn, her leg was in bad shape, and she could barely walk.

Then one day, a neighbor suggested that she attend a church service to receive prayer for her injured knee. As Yin told me, "I had been praying to find the one true God all these years, but I didn't know where I would find him." As she sat in that church service in the refugee camp, listening to the stories of Yesu, she remembered the words of her grandmother. Yesu had been pierced in his hands, feet, and side—"the design of a disk," the "stab wound," the "marks like scars" on his forehead. "Until that moment," Yin recalled, "I didn't know his name was Yesu." Then she heard how Yesu had overcome death, and she knew that he was the true God she had been seeking since she was a young girl, the "golden boat" who would carry her to heaven.

That night, Yin dreamed about Jesus—his hands were pierced, and he was holding out a ruby, the most valuable gemstone in Cambodia. When she awoke, she wondered if she would accept his gift. Then the Cambodian pastor at the church in the refugee camp invited Yin to be baptized. "We will walk to the waterfall and climb down the riverbank to baptize you and the other new believers in the river. Are you ready?"

Yin knew she had been praying to Jesus her whole life. She believed he had delivered her from the Khmer Rouge, and she wanted to accept the ruby he had held out to her in her dream, but she wasn't sure she could climb down the riverbank with her painful leg. "Then we will carry you," the pastor said. He and his wife carried Yin down the steep slope of the riverbank, and she was baptized in the rushing water. She had found the One God that her grandmother had told her about so many times. By the end of that week, Yin's leg was fully healed, and she was grateful for another answered prayer.

I marveled at this story of transformation, so rooted in Khmer Buddhism, and so unique to the experience of a Khmer Rouge survivor. I began to wonder about the other ways that God had been revealing himself through local cultures and religions around the world.

FIND REDEMPTIVE ANALOGIES

The Canadian missionary Don Richardson moved with his wife, Carol, and their young son to live as outsider-seekers among the Sawi people in Papua New Guinea—a headhunting tribe of cannibalistic warriors. As a linguist, Don spent many years learning the language and culture of the community. The Sawi language was daunting in its complexity, with nineteen tenses for every verb. But with a rigorous schedule of language study for eight to ten hours a day, Don eventually became proficient.

The Sawi culture was even more challenging to understand, and Don grew discouraged as he watched the way the tribe interacted with their rivals, as they seemed to value treachery and deception above love and neighborliness. When Don told them about the life of Jesus, they seized on the character of Judas Iscariot and hailed him as a hero for his traitorous behavior. "In their eyes, Judas, not Jesus, was the hero of the Gospels. Jesus was just the dupe to be laughed at."[4]

Nevertheless, Don continued to love and seek to discover the goodness of God in the Sawi people. One day, after living among the Sawi for several years, their village was attacked by an enemy tribe. After weeks of fighting, the Richardsons were almost ready to give up and go back to Canada. Life among the Sawi was just too violent, and breakthroughs seemed nonexistent.

But after a particularly brutal week of fighting that ended with heavy casualties, the Sawi tribal chief called together everyone in the village, along with a delegation from the enemy tribe, to attend an important ceremony. With pomp and formality, the chief rose and stood in front of the gathered crowd. His eyes were filled with sorrow as he took his own infant son and placed him in the arms of the opposing chief. This ancient tribal ritual had been passed down from one generation of Sawi to the next, and the Sawi people called this child "the Peace Child."

The chief had paid the ultimate price for peace—his own son would live with his adversaries for the rest of his life. In this way, there could be peace between the tribes. Don wrote: "If a man would actually give his own son to his enemies, that man could be trusted!"[5]

As Don pondered this remarkable turn of events, he recognized the clear fingerprints of God in this ancient practice. He began to consult with tribal members, exploring the connection between what the chief had done in offering his infant son so there could be peace for his people and how Jesus, the Son of God, had given his life to bring an end to death and violence for the whole world. This insight led to beautiful moments of common understanding and growing faith within the Sawi tribe.

Don called this cultural touchpoint a "redemptive analogy,"[6] and he observed how these redemptive analogies are widely used in Scripture. For example, the Jewish people sacrificed lambs as a way of seeking forgiveness for their sins. Thus, when Jesus arrived on the scene, John the Baptist said, "Look, the Lamb of God, who takes away the sin of the world!" (Jn 1:29). This redemptive analogy was a bridge that enabled the Jews to perceive immediately who Jesus was—and what he had come to do.

As Don Richardson reflected on these redemptive analogies, he became convinced that cultures everywhere already have connecting points for the gospel of Jesus. This approach, of course, reflects the time-honored strategy of using what is already known to introduce what is unknown. Our role, then, as outsider-seekers is simply to discover, and join, the conversation God is already having with someone.

Look for God's Fingerprints

These redemptive analogies do not need to be some mind-blowing discovery in an ancient religious text or widely held cultural legend. If we open our eyes and hearts to seek God in each place and culture, we will begin to see his fingerprints all around us. This is how outsider evangelists become seekers.

After a storm at Shalom Valley, a massive tree fell onto its side, but rather than dying and decaying, the tree began to flourish and grow right where it had fallen. Phearom saw this tree and invited a small group of young people to gather around it and consider the ways of God, who brings goodness and life out of suffering and death.

As I stood in holy silence with this group of young Cambodians, I noticed an Alongsiders leader wiping tears from her cheeks. She pulled me aside later to explain, "Craig, that moment of silence standing by the fallen tree was like a balm for my soul. A few months ago, two young girls were kidnapped and murdered in my village. When I came to this retreat, I was on the verge of depression and giving up. But standing by that fallen tree, I prayed that life would come from death, and I recommitted myself to training up more Alongsiders to walk alongside and protect vulnerable children."

The bomb crater at Shalom Valley was another ideal place to invite small groups of young people to leave their comfort zones and open their eyes, ears, and hearts to encounter the God who brings shalom. Many nights, as we sat together talking, laughing, and crying in the crater under the stars, surrounded by earth movers and rock piles from all the construction, we encountered the powerful alchemy of God's redemption emerging in that place.

The story of Jesus reveals the upside-down kingdom that God wants to establish on earth, the vision of God's shalom in our midst. During my time walking through the streets of Vancouver's Downtown Eastside, I had learned how annoying it was to hear a canned presentation of the gospel. Very few people want to listen to a rote list of four spiritual laws that some stranger presents as truth without any opportunity for mutual learning. Yet plenty of people are interested in swapping stories with a friend.

I remember sitting late into the night with about a dozen Alongsiders and their friends, and several people began telling stories that had been passed down from parents and grandparents about the Khmer Rouge days. The violence of that period is still raw for most Cambodians, even those who were born after the war. Many young people suffer secondary trauma from their older relatives, but they lack safe spaces to share and process their feelings.

That night, we talked about the distorted vision of the Khmer Rouge for a radical new peasant society, one where there would be no families, and relationships would only serve the nation state. We talked about how small children were encouraged to report on their parents, how husbands and wives were supposed to spy on each other.

The group grew quiet as they reckoned once more with the damage that the revolution had done to trusting relationships within their homes and villages—damage that had continued to ripple into their lives more than forty years later. As I listened to these young people discussing the secondary trauma they had experienced from the Khmer Rouge, I became a learner all over again.

Remembering Paulo Freire's words—"Whoever teaches, learns in the act of teaching, and whoever learns, teaches in the act of learning"[7]—I began to wonder what good news Jesus might have for this situation. Since God welcomes us all into his family, no one will be rejected, no one will be excluded, no one will be abandoned or unloved. This is the promise of God's shalom.

I knew that some in the group had lost their parents or grandparents to the Khmer Rouge, and others had lost loved ones to family brokenness and divorce. The love feast of Jesus, where everyone would be invited and no one would be excluded, seemed like radically good news for these Cambodian young people.

Looking around the group, I asked, "Who did the Khmer Rouge kill first?"

"People with glasses," several said at once. Someone nudged their neighbor, who was wearing glasses, and we all laughed, allowing the dark humor to break the tension.

"Right," I said, "because they wanted to get rid of anyone with education so they could start a peasant revolution with simple farmers." I motioned toward those wearing glasses. "You would be dead—and you and you . . ." My voice trailed off. For the next few moments, we sat together in silence.

Then we began to talk about how the Khmer Rouge had hated academic knowledge but loathed wisdom even more. Because they had destroyed an entire generation of leaders, professionals, and academics, there were very few trained and experienced leaders to help rebuild the country. To make matters even worse, the Khmer Rouge leaders didn't know how to farm rice properly, and they set up their irrigation gullies according to longitude and latitude instead of following the natural contours of the land. Their rice yields were much lower, costing them dearly and leading to widespread famine throughout the country. We all fell quiet once more, thinking of the hundreds of thousands of people who had died because of this ignorance.

I prayed silently, listening to the gentle rustle of the bamboo leaves nearby, and then asked, "So, if the Khmer Rouge was bad news for Cambodia, what might God's good news look like?"

We talked late into the night, swapping stories, swatting mosquitoes, and sharing our dreams about how we might work together to carry out God's vision for shalom in Cambodia.

7

DANGER #3
SECULARISM

Enter a river where it bends, enter a land by its customs.

CAMBODIAN PROVERB

I DROVE FROM Shalom Valley back to Phnom Penh, and when I arrived in our neighborhood, the kids came chattering and crowding into our house to play with LEGO bricks, as usual. A couple of them were carrying Roxy, and as they propped her up in the corner like a rag doll, they told me she was sick, and then began to play.

Roxy remained listless and quiet in the corner. When I called her name, she slowly moved her head toward me, but I could see that she could not move her limbs. When I bent to lift her, her legs swung beneath her, and she felt as light as an empty rice sack.

I held Roxy to my chest and asked her older sister, Diamond, what was wrong. Diamond shrugged. "She can't walk right now." Sickness and death were commonplace in this community.

I left the kids with the LEGO bricks and carried Roxy around the corner to the dimly lit room where her family lived, all crammed together. Our houses shared a back wall, but Roxy's had no furniture other than a dirty mattress on the floor and piles of dirty clothes in the corners. The walls were grimy and water stained.

I stood in the doorway, blocking most of the light. "What is wrong with Roxy?" I asked her mother, who turned a tear-stained face to look up at me. "I don't know . . . she hasn't been walking for a few days now. I don't know what to do."

"We can take her to a clinic if you like." As I shifted Roxy to the other hip, her mother nodded and indicated that she would stay back.

I propped Roxy on the back of my motorbike between my daughter, Micah, and Diamond, then rode up through the alley and out onto the main road. It was getting dark, and I was worried we wouldn't find an open clinic.

Eventually, we saw the bright, fluorescent lights of a clinic illuminating the dusky street. A white-clad nurse looked up from her computer as we came in, and soon Roxy was lying on a mattress in a stark back room. A doctor came to examine her and placed a stethoscope to Roxy's tiny chest as she labored to breathe. Diamond and Micah held Roxy's hands, one on each side of the bed.

Then the doctor sat back and sighed. "She's malnourished. That's why her legs have stopped working," he said in thickly accented English, though I had explained her situation in Khmer.

"Aha," I nodded somberly. "What can we do?"

"I will put her on the IV drip and give you a prescription that will help her to begin walking in a couple of days. Give her lots of rice porridge, fruits, and vegetables. Okay, sir?"

Roxy barely even winced when he jabbed her in the arm with a needle for the IV. Then the doctor gave us a little plastic bag filled with medicine, and we took her home.

I carried Roxy back into her room and laid her on the mat next to her mother. Then I gave her mother the medicine and passed on the doctor's instructions, promising to come back the next day to see how she was. By now, it was late, so Micah and I walked back to our own home next door. "I hope she's okay, Dad," Micah whispered. I squeezed her hand. "Me too, darling."

The following day, I heard a commotion from the alleyway, so I drifted over. The neighbors were crowded around Roxy's doorway, and I couldn't see.

"Roxy's mother hired a fortuneteller to treat Roxy's sickness," one of the older women told me. Then she told me how much it had cost—money that she likely borrowed from another neighbor—and I winced.

Everyone had gathered in the doorway to watch the incantation, which included chanting and blowing on Roxy while swaying and waving around some lucky amulets. I heard the familiar melodic prayer chant that monks and fortunetellers across Cambodia had perfected, a nasal rhythm and cadence that was neither singing nor talking. I shook my head and went back into my house.

A day later, I went to visit again and was delighted to see that Roxy was looking much better. She was standing and even walking tentatively around the room. Her mother was ecstatic. "Look at my daughter, she's walking! The fortuneteller's magic worked!"

I rolled my eyes, rudely betraying my frustration, and stormed back to my house. At home, Nay was reading a book, but she put it down when I stomped in. "Can you believe what Roxy's mother is saying?" I spluttered. "The IV drip, the medicine I bought her, the doctor's treatment—none of that meant anything! As far as she was concerned, it was some magic blowing and expensive chanting that healed Roxy! Next time she gets sick, she can figure it out with the fortuneteller herself!"

Nay looked at me a second and then laughed. "You're right. It was a waste of money, and she can barely feed her children, but you and I both know she just wants Roxy to get better. And if she believes the evil spirits caused Roxy's sickness, then her remedy will be spiritual too. That's why she cuts her kids' hair wonky and changes their names every now and then—to confuse the spirits."

I realized once again how much I had to learn about this culture—and how secular my own worldview was. My Western instincts had led me to trust fully and completely in modern medicine. Though I acknowledged medical care as a gift from God, my approach to health and healing would be barely discernible from that of anyone in the West, both believers and nonbelievers. I recognized that I was a thoroughly secularized Christian and that if I were to become more of a seeker, I had much more to learn from my Cambodian neighbors.

CHRISTIANS WHO SECULARIZE

Throughout much of the non-Western world—even in "developed" nations such as South Korea and Singapore—there is a more holistic approach to life and health. Yet, over the past two centuries, some anthropologists point out that Western missionaries have been a major source of secularization throughout Asia and Africa.[1] If theology combines beliefs with actual practice, then Westerners have a very compartmentalized faith. Our beliefs and actions are often treated as two entirely separate things. As seekers, our role is not to reject science but to recognize that it doesn't explain everything. In church, we preach passionately about the spiritual realm, but as soon as we are faced with a crisis—whether physical, economic, political, or social—we fall back on what we can see and touch.

Troubled about my secular perspective, I asked Phearom to help me understand more about the Khmer spiritual worldview. I knew he had grappled with these issues a lot because the area around Shalom Valley had been used as a Chinese graveyard for several decades and was thought to be haunted by ghosts. Chinese Cambodians would come several times a year to maintain the graves and appease their ancestors with offerings of incense, chicken, and cans of Tiger beer. If they neglected these rituals, they believed they would run the risk of angering the ghosts, which could bring bad luck on their family fortunes.

Phearom told me that elders from the village had advised him to make offerings to the ancestors at Shalom Valley before we opened the camp, and they said that we should fear the ghosts of those who had been killed by the American bombing campaign. Phearom had reassured the elders that Jesus was more powerful than the ghosts, so we had nothing to worry about. As the Cambodian proverb says, "One mountain cannot have two tigers." We quoted this a lot to explain why we only offer our worship to the one true God.

To help me understand Roxy's mother, Phearom told me how his aunt (who had adopted him) had made money from a side hustle as a fortuneteller. "Local people used to pay her to deal with all kinds of ailments and curses," he said. "They even brought demon-possessed people to her for exorcisms. The scariest encounter I ever had with this realm was my stepsister, Srepo, who came home from school one day when she was seventeen, complaining that there was some kind of demon inside her, attempting to throw her into the lake and drown her. She was screaming, and when I came out to the porch, I found her holding onto a post and crying that her legs were being lifted and pulled away."

"Phearom," I said, pushing back, "did Srepo struggle with mental illness?"

"Perhaps," he said, agreeing. "She experienced rejection from her biological father and struggled in various ways, but there was definitely a spiritual component too. She started eating only raw beef and sleeping all day. People were afraid to look her in the eyes because they seemed to drill deep into their soul." He shook his head. "It was really spooky. Then one night, my aunt woke me up with her screams, and I found Srepo with both hands around my aunt's neck, trying to strangle her. It was like something out of a horror movie."

I gulped. "Holy smokes. What did you do?"

"I managed to calm her down and get her away from my aunt," he said. "But after that, my aunt began burning incense day and night, and she brought in several more traditional healers and fortunetellers. One warned us that he couldn't do anything because this demon was too strong. He said we should be very, very afraid. On his way home, he was in a serious traffic accident."

Phearom took a deep breath, and I began to feel a bit queasy. "In the end," he continued, "my aunt had to borrow money from the loan sharks to pay all these traditional healers. After several months, she was $2500 in debt, and nothing had worked. Then she finally allowed me to bring Srepo to the church for prayer. We couldn't bring her to a normal church service during the day because the demon wouldn't let her outside in the daylight, so we brought her in the evening."

Phearom closed his eyes and shivered. "I still have this vivid memory of the song we sang that night—'Every time I pray, God moves in power.' As we sang the words, her hand started shaking violently, and then a deep, masculine voice came from her mouth and started taunting us, 'Do you think you can destroy us with this song?'"

Though the night air was cool, sweat started to trickle down my back as Phearom continued remembering that night. "We started praying hard in Jesus' name for the demon to leave, believing that Jesus had power over the spiritual realm—and after that night, she started to improve bit by bit. Within a few months, she was fully recovered and back in school. She's never had any trouble like that again."

He shook his head and then looked straight into my eyes. "You know what else?"

I had no idea what else he might have to add to this story, which was freaking me out more and more.

"She's a believer in Jesus and an Alongsider now, with a little sister."

I whistled through my teeth and grinned. "That story was quite the roller coaster, Phearom."

Phearom laughed and explained that his experience with his stepsister had helped him mentor young people when they were struggling with fear or dark spiritual activity. "A few weeks ago, at the Shalom Valley construction site," he continued, "one of the volunteers saw a shadow that seemed to be laughing and mocking him, so he ran to me for help."

As I listened to Phearom's story, I realized that my first instinct would have been to reassure the boy that there is no such thing as ghosts. Like most Westerners, I tended to default to the scientific and secular interpretation of events.

But Phearom told me how he took the boy to the book of Isaiah, and they read and prayed against the spirits together:

So do not fear, for I am with you;
   do not be dismayed, for I am your God.
I will strengthen you and help you;
   I will uphold you with my righteous right hand.
      (Is 41:10)

As secularized outsider-seekers, we have a lot to learn from cultures that are more holistic. For most Asians, Africans, and Latinos, the spiritual, physical, emotional, social, and political worlds are intricately intertwined. Physical well-being cannot be separated from mental well-being, and both are connected with spiritual well-being.

Contending with Powers and Principalities

A few weeks after my conversation with Phearom, he told me that the local police had been visiting Shalom Valley on a daily basis to shake us down for bribes. "Last week they came three times a day and stayed for an hour or more," he told me. "They are heavily armed, and sometimes it's obvious that they've been drinking."

I was incensed. What right did these thugs have to come around and demand bribes? We had tried to do everything by the book. We'd submitted hundreds of pages of documentation and building plans. We'd jumped through hoops for rezoning. And time after time, someone would withhold a signature or "lose" our papers. It was a frustrating mess, and I was starting to wonder if we would be able to get the proper permissions before our grand opening.

Our three Khmer leaders, Phearom, Marea, and Pon, were dealing with these visits with great patience and wisdom, and they often reminded me of these words from Paul's letter to the Ephesians: "For our struggle is not against flesh and blood, but against the rulers, against the authorities, against the powers of this dark world and against the spiritual forces of evil in the heavenly realms" (Eph 6:12).

Their ability to see beyond the surface was inspiring, but I knew that they were stressed out by the police harassment, so I turned to the life of Jesus to try to make sense of this complex mixture of spiritual, political, and physical opposition. In Luke 8, Jesus encounters a demon-possessed man who "had not worn clothes or lived in a house, but had lived in the tombs" (Lk 8:27). The description reminded me of some of the homeless folks I had encountered on the streets of Phnom Penh or the Downtown Eastside of Vancouver, where many people made their homes by rat-infested dumpsters in back alleys, driven to the edges by police patrols and neighborhood watch groups.

We tend to banish those who make us uncomfortable with their brokenness. The poor hold up a mirror to our most uncomfortable truths, prompting us to push them to the ragged edges of our communities so we won't have to face our own failures and addictions.[2] This is what we mean when we say someone is "marginalized"—they have been banished to the margins.

How can we be Good Samaritans if we're not willing to go to the kind of streets where people get beaten up? And how can we encounter marginalized people if we're not willing to go to the margins?

When Jesus sets foot in the land where this demon-possessed man is living, the man runs out to greet the visitors. When he sees Jesus, he cries out and falls at his feet, shouting at the top of his voice, "What do you want with me, Jesus, Son of the Most High God?" (Lk 8:28).

As I read through this story with our struggles at Shalom Valley in mind, I realized that there was a lot more going on than a simple exorcism or even mental illness. The encounter takes place just outside the Decapolis, a Roman outpost, where a bunch of military veterans (former Roman soldiers) lived on conquered lands that had been given to them as payment for their service. In light of this colonial context, it is not surprising that Jesus laces this story with military imagery.

When Jesus asks the demon for his name, he replies, "Legion," which is the Latin term for a division of Roman soldiers. For the Jews in Palestine, Legion was the face of the occupying forces. Throughout the land, the notorious Tenth Legion was known for their mascot, which was a pig.

In traditional societies, demon possession can be a socially acceptable form of protest against—or mental escape from—oppression or colonialism. So, in one sense, the occupation of this man's body by a demonic force named Legion can also be understood as a subversive middle finger raised to the legions of the Roman Empire, which had conquered and then possessed this man's land. For local peasants living under Roman rule, these satirical undercurrents in the story would have been obvious.

Then Jesus confronts the powers and the principalities, making it clear that our battle is not against flesh and blood. He does not ignore the political powers by claiming that the only solution we need is a change of heart, but he also does not ignore the spiritual powers by trying to raise up a revolutionary army to bring a change of guard. Instead, he engages in a theatrical act of subversion.

Jesus casts the demons out of the man and into a nearby herd of pigs, who are loitering around, feeding off the land. At the command of Jesus, these pigs leave the occupied land immediately, rushing headlong, screeching and squealing, into the water. Thus, the legion are symbolically, spiritually, and physically cast from their colonized land and drowned in the sea.

As I reflected on this story, I sensed that there was a deeper lesson for us at Shalom Valley. We were under constant siege from the local authorities, battling over the land, and seeking the shalom of this valley, a place that Phearom, Pon, and Marea were trying to reclaim for the children of Cambodia. Yet our struggle was not only against flesh and blood—the local police. Like the Tenth Legion, they were just cogs in the system of corruption and political power games. We were contending with bigger powers and principalities that were working to deter us from God's vision of shalom for this valley and all of Cambodia.

As we reflected together on Ephesians 6 and Jesus' encounter with the demoniac in Luke 8, Phearom invited us all to pray for the eyes of the local police to be opened and also for a breakthrough in the spiritual realm. We knew that we desperately needed this breakthrough if we were going to open Shalom Valley in a few months.

SUPERNATURAL HEALING

Soon after this conversation with Phearom, Pon, and Marea, the children in my neighborhood carried Roxy to our house again. Since the night we had taken Roxy to the clinic, I had gained a reputation for being concerned about their physical well-being, so they enjoyed showing me their various cuts and bruises. This time, Roxy's foot had a mildly infected cut, a result of walking barefoot through the muddy slum in the rainy season. Small cuts could turn into vicious infections because the nearby sewer, which was covered with thick black sludge and a layer of trash, was prone to overflow when the wastewater system was overloaded with rain.

I gathered the children around me, and as we sat on the floor of my kitchen, I opened my first-aid kit. We cleaned up Roxy's wound, and I showed them how to apply disinfectant and wipe the wound with a clean tissue. Then I raised my hands for quiet and asked them if they were ready for the main healing action. I was aiming for a theatrical act of subversion.

Wide-eyed, they nodded their heads, wondering what was about to happen. I gently pulled Roxy's foot into the very center of the circle, and then I explained, "Jesus gave us wisdom to use medicine for healing. Medicine and doctors are good, and they can help us, but Jesus is the healer above every other healer. He is the doctor above every other doctor. He has the power to heal us, so if you get sick, you can ask Jesus to help."

The children nodded enthusiastically, so I asked them, "Shall we pray to Jesus, the God above all other gods?" They nodded again, though I suspected they didn't know what it meant to pray to Jesus.

"Stretch your hands out toward Roxy's foot without touching it. You can say what I am about to say anytime you like. You don't need me to say it—and you don't need to pay anyone to say it, okay?"

Then I began to chant a very simple Khmer chant, which anyone who has heard Buddhist monks or Khmer fortunetellers would recognize. It had a nasal rhythm and a cadence that is neither singing nor talking, and the words were very simple. We chanted them several times:

In the name of Jesus Christ, our healer, please bring healing. Thank you, God.

The children were captivated by the simplicity and power of this prayer, the first prayer they had learned to say themselves without relying on paid "holy men." They now had direct access to the God who loves and heals them. It felt right to empower them and give them a tool that would allow them to take one step out of a system that was keeping them poor—not by replacing that system with reliance on me but by pointing them to God, who seeks them in ways that they can understand.

8

FROM PASTOR (INSIDER) TO MIDWIFE (OUTSIDER)

When you can put your church on the back of my camel then I will think that Christianity is meant for us Somalis.

CAMEL HERDER, NORTHERN KENYA

THOUGH LIVING IN OUR VIBRANT little tin-roof slum was a joy and privilege, it was becoming unsustainable for our family. Our two children had to sit in a stuffy taxi van as they wove through chaotic traffic for an hour each way across the city to get to their school, where Nay was also teaching three days a week to supplement our income. As our life was torn between these two ends of the city, we knew that something had to give. Nay and I talked late into the night about the decision to move.

By living in this community for the past four years, we had imagined that we were somehow symbolically following in the footsteps of Jesus, who had left the most exclusive gated community in the universe to move into the neighborhood and walk alongside us: "Peace [*shalom*] to you! As the Father has sent Me, I also send you" (Jn 20:21 NKJV).

But if we were honest, we also had to acknowledge that our joy had always been tinged with sorrow. Roxy's family continued to struggle, and we were scared for her future as well as Diamond's. We also saw many more of our neighbors becoming involved in drug activity. Though we had gotten used to seeing used needles on the ground in the Downtown Eastside of Vancouver, we'd never expected to see that in Cambodia. But pain is universal, and addiction is universal too. Its forms just vary from place to place.

After many late-night conversations, we discussed the idea of moving to the other side of the city with our kids, closer to their school but, sadly, far away from the neighbors we had grown to love. Soon, we were saying our tearful goodbyes to Diamond, Roxy, and the rest of our little community and loading up our belongings in the rusty old truck we'd hired to carry us to the other side of town. I would grieve the loss of this close-knit community for a long time. We knew that our privilege allowed us to move when our neighbors had far fewer options.

We ended up in a more mixed-income neighborhood known as Two Tigers. The entrance to the community was on a dusty side road that was "guarded" by two crudely constructed, life-sized, concrete tigers whose tails had been snapped off over the years, leaving them with gaping holes at the back.

We moved into a narrow dirt lane, which was dotted on each side with a mixture of corrugated iron shacks, three-story rooming apartments, and middle-class row houses. There was even a villa, which looked quite grand, but then I peeked through the gate and saw rows of young women sitting behind sewing machines. We never did see many of them coming or going. They sewed long hours, seven days a week, and slept on the floor.

When we met the landlord to pick up the keys for our new house, he unlocked the front door, immediately walked over to the little altar in the corner of the room, lit some incense, and knelt and prayed solemnly to the territorial spirit that many Khmer believe protects every house. Then he rose to his feet and asked if we wanted to keep the altar. I let him know that we wouldn't need it. "One mountain cannot have two tigers," I quipped. "Jesus is our Guardian Spirit." I was amused by how the Khmer proverb had just taken on a brand-new meaning in that community known as Two Tigers.

Releasing Control

As we approached the official opening of Shalom Valley and anticipated receiving hundreds of Alongsiders and their little brothers and little sisters, everyone was getting excited.

Though Mart-Jan, the bespectacled Dutch engineer, had been working around the clock with Pon and the construction team to complete the buildings before the launch, we still had no official building permits—just a verbal "thumbs-up" from a local leader. This meant the police could technically shut down construction at any moment.

Both Phearom and Mart-Jan, who were co-leading different aspects of the building project, had recently relocated to Kep so they could be closer to Shalom Valley. In traditional mission work, outsiders typically start a ministry and place themselves in leadership roles, then gradually pass on that mantle to local people. Yet this process of "nationalization" or "localization" rarely results in true ownership by local people. Through our years in Cambodia, we had learned that it was much better to help local leaders birth something themselves, which they could fully own and shape from the beginning. This is the core difference between being an insider pastor and an outsider midwife.

▼ THE MIDWIFE ◢

Midwives are pastorally gifted leaders who nurture and protect the people of God, helping insiders birth and care for communities of faith. As outsiders, they are passionate about cultivating the local church and developing disciples without needing to be in the limelight. They are careful to use church-planting methods, together with local shepherds, that can be replicated without outside resources.

When people from so-called developed countries come to help in areas that they perceive as impoverished, we carry the baggage of privilege. This can include a lack of confidence in local people's ability to think and make decisions for themselves. Though it is often packed tightly into a hidden corner of a suitcase, this is the false savior mindset—a pattern of dominance. Though many of us truly want to see transformation, deep down we are tempted to believe that we must be the executors of that transformation. Instead of demonstrating the fruit of self-control, we seek to control others.

Though we may talk a big game about empowerment, if we're honest, we struggle to trust the local leaders. Yet trusting local leaders is one of the most important ingredients in the recipe for change, especially in contexts that have a traumatic history of mistrust. True servants can be identified in the way that they trust other people rather than insisting on serving others through a million acts of benevolence that are performed without real trust.

In attempting to forge a different pathway, we were accompanying Phearom as he prepared to take the helm of Shalom Valley with a stake in ownership. Mart-Jan's role was that of "shadow leader,"[1] whose focus would be on Phearom rather than himself so that Phearom could grow into leadership before the camp opened. We had already discussed how it is only by making decisions that we can learn to decide,[2] but there was a steep learning curve for both of them. Phearom had never run a business, and Mart-Jan was learning how to be intentional about empowering local leaders and staying in the background.

Throughout this time, Pon and Mart-Jan had also been journeying with some local believers who had asked them to start a Bible study after the local church closed down. Phearom soon joined them, and the group rotated between different people's homes in the community. Phearom and Mart-Jan were seeking to nurture authentic Cambodian disciples who would follow Jesus and become a grassroots faith community in the seaside town of Kep.

Though most of the new team forming at Shalom Valley were followers of Jesus, Phearom had hired Mow, a dynamic young

Muslim woman from a nearby village, to work in the kitchen. The name *Mow*, which means "black" in Khmer, is commonly bestowed on babies with darker skin. She had bright eyes and wasn't afraid to speak up or make friends. As a child, Mow had spent a year outside Cambodia undergoing Islamic instruction at a madrasa in Malaysia. She quickly became a lively part of the Shalom Valley team.

When Mow heard Phearom and Marea talking about a Bible study at Phearom's house, she asked if she could come. "Of course," Phearom said, "but would your mother mind? She was not too happy about you working here in the first place."

Mow insisted that it wouldn't be a problem, and that night she showed up at Phearom's house. She sat with Marea and was immediately drawn to the singing. "I've never heard songs like this before," she said. "There is something about this Jesus that makes me feel peaceful."

Mow joined in the discussions, fascinated and vocal. At the end of the study, she vowed to come back. "This Jesus is not like other gods," she said. "This Jesus—*Isu*—is special," she said, using the word used by local Islamic communities to identify Jesus.

Later, I asked Phearom about his decision to host the Bible study at his house rather than Shalom Valley. He said that because Shalom Valley was a business that would provide jobs and livelihood for staff, it would not be an ideal location for a church. If someone were fired from Shalom Valley, that person, along with their relatives and friends, would all stop coming to any church service that was held onsite. Others might attend the church in the hopes of gaining employment with Shalom Valley.

Phearom felt that it was wiser and more sustainable to keep a clear distance between the business, the NGO, and the church.

In seeking wisdom about how to pastor a fledgling church in Cambodia, we were convinced that we needed to rediscover the original meaning of our English translation of "pastor." In Greek the word *poimēn* is translated into the English word *pastor* only once in the New Testament.[3] Elsewhere it is always translated as "shepherd," as in "I am the good shepherd" (Jn 10:11).

Yet, in the West many churches have taken the fivefold ministry roles that Paul outlines in Ephesians (apostle, prophet, evangelist, pastor, and teacher) and rolled them all into pastor, which tellingly often looks like the CEO of a corporation. In most non-Western contexts, the Western idea of a pastor as a CEO—especially when there is an outsider in that role—is simply a throwback to colonialism.

Those of us who had grown up in the West knew that we needed to take off our Western church glasses and see the pastor role as it was supposed to be—not as a CEO, big boss man, or chief but as a sheep herder who leads gently from behind, gathering, nurturing, and protecting the flock from enemy attack. We wanted to look to Jesus as our role model for a pastor-shepherd.

In Psalm 23, the good shepherd uses a staff and a rod to care for the sheep. These tools are used for gently guiding and nudging the sheep and also for beating off any vicious animals that might attack the flock. The shepherd-pastor's role is to provide gentle guidance from behind the scenes along with protection for the flock.

I grew up in New Zealand, the land with thirty million sheep—literally, six white woolly sheep for every lucky man, woman, and child in the country. But even so, like most Kiwis, I did not grow up with my six sheep bleating and pooping right there in my backyard, and I am not super familiar with what it means to be a shepherd. For outsiders like myself, it may be more helpful to use a different metaphor, one that may be slightly more familiar to many of us—that of a midwife. The term *midwife* can help us reimagine our role as helpers in "birthing" new things in a crosscultural context instead of acting as the central players.

Midwives are at work almost everywhere in the world, from hospitals to natural birthing centers to homes, particularly in Asia and Africa, where traditional midwives (usually wise old women) play an important role in the community by attending the births of women who are too poor to go to the hospital. Like the subversive Hebrew midwives, Shiphrah and Puah, who disobeyed the Pharaoh's order to kill the Hebrew sons (Ex 1:15-22), midwives around the world save lives every day as they accompany mothers through labor, assist them during the birthing process, and offer follow-up support after the birth. The role of the midwife is always changing, depending on the experience and confidence of the mother. A newbie mother may need a whole lot of handholding, reassurance, and guidance. An experienced mother may only need help if something goes wrong.

Whereas a CEO-pastor is often revered as the star of the service or the hero of a congregation, a midwife humbly and gently comes behind a congregation, helping people tend one another's needs.

Whereas a CEO-pastor typically wears an expensive suit and sits in the front row—all eyes on him (and it is usually *him*, isn't it?)—the midwife blends into the congregation and supports from the side, pointing all eyes to Jesus.

Whereas a CEO-pastor takes the microphone and hogs the limelight because the stage, honor, credit, and glory are his, a midwife knows she is not the main act. She puts others first and helps others birth the vision that God has placed within them.

Whereas a CEO-pastor makes all the decisions and calls all the shots, a midwife encourages others to participate in decision making and lifts up the voice of those who are often overlooked.

The world does not need more CEO-pastors going out as missionaries to take center stage and eventually—eventually!—hand over their precious baby to locals. This is the benevolent outsider approach. In contrast, in the upside-down kingdom, God is raising up outsider midwives who will commit to serve from the sidelines, to let go of power in order to empower others to lead. God is the only one who can birth any new initiative: "Unless the LORD builds the house, / the builders labor in vain" (Ps 127:1).

CONTEXTUALIZING WORSHIP

In Cambodia, the first missionaries saw Khmer people burning sticks of incense each day to worship their ancestors and appease the local spirits. Overlooking the fact that God commanded his people to use incense for worship in the Old

Testament,[4] the missionaries perceived this centuries-old local practice to be closely tied to heathen rituals, so they banned it. This ban became an ongoing point of pain and tension between Cambodian Christians and their families and neighbors. Instead of using incense and other traditional practices to worship Jesus, Cambodian Christians have been left with poorly translated music from Hillsong and Bethel, Western melodies and concepts that sound strange to Cambodian ears.

As Swazi theologian Dr. B. Makhatini says,

> Christianity is the bread of life for all races. When Europeans received this bread they added a plastic bag [i.e., their own customs]. Later when the European missionaries arrived in Africa they fed us the plastic bag along with the bread. The plastic bag makes us sick! The plastic belongs to them. . . . But the bread of life belongs to all of us. We can remove the plastic, and enjoy the bread.[5]

Because this "plastic bag" comes with the bread, local believers are seen as followers of a foreign god who regularly angers the spirit world and calls them to deny their own culture.

Just try to imagine what would happen if a group of Cambodian missionaries relocated to New York and set up a church using traditional Khmer instruments, such as the *kongvong*, and all the songs were based on the pentatonic (five-note) musical scale found throughout Asia. The words to these songs would be translated into English from the original Khmer language and would describe the rice harvest and the rainy season. During the worship service, all the men would sit cross-legged on the floor, and the women would sit on the floor with their knees folded to the side, Cambodian-style. Can you imagine how foreign this church would seem to most New Yorkers? And yet, that is exactly what we have done by exporting our Western forms of church and worship to other countries. Perhaps it should not be a surprise that followers of Jesus represent only around 2 percent of the population in Cambodia![6]

What might it look like to plant churches and embrace forms of worship that reflect a local culture? In Mongolia, the missionary-midwives understood that yak milk held a rich and sacred significance in Mongolian culture. After milking the yak, Mongolians would toss a cup of yak's milk into the air as an offering to the gods. When Mongolians began to follow Jesus, rather than banning the practice of tossing yak's milk to the gods, the missionaries wisely encouraged Mongolian believers to continue tossing their milk into the air with joy and abandon as an offering and act of worship to their new Lord, Jesus. Thus, a movement of Jesus-following milk-tossers was born all across Mongolia. I'm a milk-tosser. You're a milk-tosser. Everyone's a milk-tosser for Jesus! What a beautiful sight!

NURTURING PRESENCE

During a meeting at Shalom Valley one afternoon, Phearom's phone rang, and after looking at the caller ID, he immediately picked it up. "Hello, sister Mow? Are you okay?" he asked, his face creased with concern. Mow had fainted at Shalom Valley the day before, and she'd gone home early to rest in bed. A virus was spreading in her village after three men had returned from an Islamic conference in Malaysia, and the whole team was worried.

"I don't think I'll be able to come to work today," Mow whispered into the phone. "I can't get up from bed."

Phearom urged Mow to get to a clinic for treatment. After he hung up, Marea said, "I'll go with her. She's going to need someone to help." Marea took Mow to the clinic and slept in a chair beside her bed. Presence, prayer, accompaniment: these simple, everyday acts of love and service are activities that anybody can replicate.

When Mow returned to work a few days later, she was smiling and joking around with the rest of the team as usual. That afternoon, she joined our weekly time of worship. As we handed bread and juice to one another, sharing Communion as a large group, Marea explained the meaning of each element, remembering what Jesus had done for us by overcoming death and sickness. When Mow picked up the bread, broke it, and placed a small piece in her mouth, her face crinkled into a cheeky smile, and her eyes shone with joy.

9

DANGER #4
MONEY

Some money is dangerous to take.

BRUCE CAIN

THE DAY FOR THE GRAND OPENING OF SHALOM VALLEY was quickly approaching, but the logistics of running the camp were growing more complicated every day. I was feeling very stretched because the grassroots Alongsiders discipleship movement had spread into more than twenty countries in Asia and Africa (including some that I had never even visited), so it was taking most of my time and focus.

As the Alongsiders movement grew, a group of young Cambodian animators and digital enthusiasts in Phnom Penh were figuring out how to use the internet to spread the vision. I was proud that the Alongsiders movements in each country were 100 percent locally led—we were truly a grassroots movement of the people, for the people. Thousands of young Christians were catching the vision to commit to encourage and disciple a vulnerable child from their community and walk alongside little brothers and little sisters until they were old enough to become Alongsiders themselves. In Cambodia, we were already seeing the fourth generation of little brothers and sisters becoming Alongsiders.

But the Alongsiders discipleship movement was very different from Shalom Valley, which was a social enterprise that needed to turn a profit—or at least break even. To make sure we weren't running at a loss, we needed proper systems and structures, which required a lot of boring policy documents.

It's almost impossible for us as Westerners to grasp the power of money in poor places—or to understand the danger of using it wrongly. But this is a major danger for those who seek to come as outsiders. When we realize how much can happen with a small cash injection, we tend to think, *Why not?* If we deal with problems by throwing cash at them in our own country, we might assume there's nothing wrong with doing so elsewhere.

Want to plant a hundred churches? It's not too hard to find a hundred impoverished Christian workers to hire as pastors. Boom! A hundred churches. Mission accomplished.

Want to feed and educate a thousand low-caste children in India? Those hundred churches will gladly take your money to help feed and educate ten children each. Boom! A thousand children fed and schooled.

Want to mobilize a thousand grassroots social workers? Boom! Your money can make that happen too.

Some might wonder, *Why not?* Change is change. Help is help. Good is good. But power and resources in the hands of outsiders can do great damage and undermine what God wants to do in the long run through local people. Injections of foreign cash disempower the local community and convey that their salvation depends on outside saviors.

AREAS OF CONCERN

As our Alongsiders leadership team reckoned with the danger of supporting the ministry with outside funds, we talked through the following four key areas of concern. These same areas of concern apply to discipleship movements, church planting, and other initiatives that need to be locally led and sustainable:

First, what happens when the money gets cut off?[1] While grappling with this issue, Compassion International and thousands of other NGOs were being forced to shut down in India due to changes in government policy that cut off the supply of funds from foreign sources.[2] Many large charities had to close or dramatically reduce their efforts when funding dried up. In our conversations, we agreed that money is not wrong in and of itself since it can be used to create opportunities that could promote ongoing sustainability (as with social enterprises). But we also agreed that it can be used to create dependency. We felt that the Shalom Valley adventure camp would need to be financially self-sustainable once it was up and running, so we decided to structure it as a business—opening up the venue to other groups who would pay for rental and food—rather than as an NGO.

Second, money distorts the relationship between the wisdom of a project and the results. We had already seen how almost any project could be started—even foolish and disempowering ones—simply because people found money to make it happen. We asked ourselves if this was a danger with the adventure camp. There would always be poor people willing to go along with a misguided project if it would provide them with a salary. In Alongsiders, we had seen that one true test of an idea is whether people are willing to embrace it first without getting paid. We didn't think that no one should ever be paid a salary, but we had learned that local ownership and passion must initiate the project and drive it forward.

Third, money concentrates power in the hands of donors instead of the poor and vulnerable. Almost everything costs something,[3] but donors should serve from the periphery rather than calling the shots. While a lot of people may agree with this statement in theory, it is very hard to practice! That's why money-fueled growth is so dangerous and common. We knew we would need to put more thought into how leadership and governance would work for a locally led adventure camp.

Fourth, using money to drive change can't be replicated by local people. If multiplication is important, as with a church plant or a discipleship movement such as Alongsiders, using outside money will create an obstacle to growth. New churches won't be easily birthed without the same cash injection. When we model methods of transformation that can't be imitated, outsiders will be perceived as the only drivers of change, a perception that further marginalizes the poor. As a team, we committed to modeling change through the Alongsiders movement. Though multiplication was less fundamental for one-off infrastructure projects or social enterprises (such as an adventure camp), we still wanted to ensure that local people would be driving the project.

MULTIPLYING DISCIPLES, NOT SUBSIDIES

In starting a Bible study with local believers, Mart-Jan and Phearom wisely decided not to rent a building for church services that local leaders could never afford. They also decided to avoid teaching English classes as an outreach activity—something local leaders could not easily replicate.[4]

Sadly, many missionaries have planted churches in ways that can't be replicated by local people. By using methods that can't be easily copied, they ensure that there will be no multiplication. When missionaries subsidize church activities with outside money, then eventually leave, the local congregation will not be able to continue gathering as a church in a self-sustaining way. The missionaries will likely be puzzled about why they have so much trouble empowering local leaders to plant more churches.

One Cambodian pastor illustrated this dynamic by telling the following story. When raising an elephant, a master will chain the elephant's leg to the base of a tree. As the elephant grows, he walks back and forth around the tree, limited by the length of chain. One day, the master takes away the chain, but the elephant retains the same limits. He never ventures further than the original length of the chain. At this point, the elephant has no physical limitations, but he continues to act as if he were chained.[5]

Many churches that have been planted by outsider-pastors behave like that trained elephant. Local leaders have only seen what has been demonstrated by the outsider-missionary pastor, but they can't copy him because they lack his access to financial and educational resources. Unless these local pastors are subsidized from the outside, they have no imagination for multiplying their churches and reaching others with the good news of Jesus. These local leaders have been set up for failure and frustration.

Even little things can make a big difference. For example, passing offering plates and baskets in church services strongly implies that people are expected to contribute cash or coins to the church.[6] Yet, in rural contexts, people may not have money, but they might have chickens or bags of rice to contribute. In the Bible, the people of God made all kinds of offerings, but our Western churches have lost that richness!

It always amazes me how Cambodians financially sustain their Buddhist religious systems even among the poorest communities. They feed the monks daily from their own household food and give both financially and through their service to maintain the pagodas, which serve as community centers that meet a wide variety of local needs.

In every nation around the world—without a single exception—the majority religion has traditionally been sustained with resources from within that country. Hinduism in Nepal does not require outside funds to keep going—nor does Islam in Senegal or Buddhism in Myanmar. And yet, so many Westerners continue to believe that missionary church plants can only survive if they are subsidized from the outside.

Jesus sent his disciples on a mission to distant lands, but he told them not to take along any possessions. He said, "Take nothing for the journey—no staff, no bag, no bread, no money, no extra shirt. Whatever house you enter, stay there until you leave that town" (Lk 9:3-4). He wanted his followers to be completely reliant on local resources and to allow local people to take the lead in providing for them. In this way, he knew that they would learn to trust God to guide them rather than depending on outsiders for their provision.

Jesus never actually told his disciples to build or plant churches, but he did command them to make disciples who would pray for his kingdom—his shalom—to come "on earth as it is in heaven" (Mt 6:9-10, Mt 28:6-20). These disciples were not meant to just recruit individuals from their existing social and familial circles so they could become part of unsustainable Christian clubrooms that would be subsidized from outside their country. Rather, these disciples were meant to transform the communities, cities, and nations that they visited so God's vision of shalom could be extended all over the world.

As Mart-Jan and Phearom slowly formed their tiny home-based, locally led discipleship group, we were filled with hope that the native plants they were tending would grow stronger and bear much wild fruit. We began to imagine together what would happen if more outsiders came into communities with a midwife mentality, a vision of walking alongside local people and sharing the gospel in ways that could be easily understood and replicated within that culture. These outsider midwives would learn the local language and hang out in places where local people could afford to gather. They would study local myths and proverbs and ask local insider pastors how these reflected or didn't reflect the shalom kingdom of God. They would ask a lot of questions about how a local person would worship Jesus, the one true God. They would empower and "shadow pastor" disciples who could lead the churches that emerged from that unique context.

FORMING COMMUNITY TABLES

For those of us who feel called to be outsider midwives, the toughest money tests often come in times of crisis—when the need is urgent and the pressure to act is suddenly upon us. Cambodia has seen more crises come and go than most countries, and during the coronavirus pandemic, the government shut down major parts of Phnom Penh on short notice.

Chaos swept the capital city as people found out about the lockdown through a Facebook leak from the prime minister's office just two hours before it went into effect. Long lines formed at supermarkets, and ATM queues stretched across the block. I jumped on my scooter and lined up with everyone else to buy some meat and nonperishables that could sustain us through the lockdown, however long it might last.

When I arrived home, Nay was sitting with our neighbor's family in the Two Tigers community. A little girl named Ning-Ning, along with her seven siblings and parents, all lived in one tiny shack just a stone's throw from our house. They had gone out to find food for the lockdown, too, but with little cash to spare, they had come home with just a couple of cans of fish and a tiny bottle of cooking oil.

"Is that all you managed to get?" Nay asked.

Ning-Ning's father shrugged his shoulders, "We don't have a fridge to store food, and besides, I didn't have any extra money to stock up."

I looked down at my bulging shopping bags with embarrassment.

The next morning, barricades had appeared at each end of our street. Police were stationed around the city, and movement outside the community was strictly forbidden. Our neighbors, who were mostly factory workers and street vendors, now had no way to earn the daily income they needed to buy food.

Seeing their struggle, Nay and I opened the fifty-kilogram sack of rice we had stored and began to divide it into bags for our neighbors. I picked up a bag and walked over to Ning-Ning's house. Nay and I had a simple rule of thumb whenever we helped our neighbors in times of emergencies: we would try to help in ways and amounts that our neighbors could replicate themselves. We didn't want to overwhelm them with our resources, but we wanted to practice generosity in simple ways that reflected and multiplied the shalom of Christ.

I wanted to share some of our food in a low-key way, without drawing attention to myself or to them. But as I arrived at Ning-Ning's little house, the plastic shopping bag full of rice caught on the corner of their bamboo bed (which was placed under a tarpaulin awning outside as a seat for the family to rest on during the heat of the day). As the rice began to pour onto the ground,

I stammered my apologies, feeling like a ridiculous white savior, while neighbors gathered around, laughing and helping to pick up the precious rice from the ground. What a failure!

Later that day, some Cambodian Alongsiders leaders gathered on Zoom to discuss how we might respond to the growing hunger crisis in our communities.

"A lot of folks are doing relief activities, distributing rice and other food," I said. "In times of real emergency, relief is a valid response," I added, sheepishly remembering my own attempt earlier that day.

"Yes, but relief supplies have to come from outside, and, besides, they are getting snapped up by those with political connections. Those who really need help are missing out," Phearom countered. "People are getting stressed out and fighting with their neighbors over the supplies."

I nodded, adjusting my webcam. "Relief activities meet a physical need, but they often bring out the worst in us. I wonder how we might love our neighbors in a more transformative way."

We tossed around a few ideas, then I mentioned something I had seen in the Philippines after they were hit by coronavirus lockdowns. "Did any of you hear about that girl in Manila who set up a table in front of her house, inviting the neighbors to add or take food, depending on their need?"

Lakhina, the media team leader who had translated *Animal Farm*, spoke up with excitement. "What if we turned that idea into a social media challenge? We could set up our own tables in front of our homes, then tag three of our friends online and challenge them to do the same!"

Now the ideas came thick and fast. We came up with a hashtag that roughly translated, "give if you have extra, help yourself if you are in need," and agreed to reconvene on Zoom the next day.

Chenda, an Alongsiders leader, asked if we could do a table together since she lived nearby. Nay and I gladly invited her to take the lead.

Chenda had been orphaned at the age of three and had grown up lonely and isolated in her community until her neighbor, a seventeen-year-old from the local church, had visited one day and asked if Chenda would like an Alongsider. Chenda didn't know what that meant, but she was drawn to her neighbor, and she blossomed under her attention until Chenda eventually became an Alongsider herself.

The next day, Chenda arrived at our house carrying some fruit and vegetables. I knew she lived in a small place and had a lot of family to support, so her gifts were truly sacrificial. Nay and Chenda set up the table and laid out a few items to share— carrots, bananas, papaya, some fish sauce, and some small bags of rice. My daughter, Micah, and her Cambodian friend Tabitha had painted a sign in Khmer: "Give if you have extra, help yourself if you are in need."

As reports began to flow in from those who participated that day, I was filled with a sense of gratitude. One widow brought a bunch of bananas to the table and took a couple of eggs. Another lady brought a pumpkin. Others brought whatever they could, and by the end of the day, everything was gone. Best of all, the divisions and fighting that often came with relief activities were transformed into a beautiful spirit of generosity and neighborly love. We had created a sustainable, locally led solution to a pressing problem. And, in the process, everyone who participated grew in dignity, knowing that they were able to contribute meaningfully.

We all posted photos on Facebook and challenged our friends to do the same. Soon, community tables began to pop up all over the city as our local friends and then strangers caught the vision. By tapping into the divine spirit of generosity that God has placed in each of us, a tiny grassroots movement sprang up during the lockdown—and then disappeared as soon as lockdown was lifted.

The use of money in contexts of poverty is fraught with danger, so we urgently need creative and sustainable ways to fund the work—whether social enterprises such as Shalom Valley or simply ministries and churches that use very little money and rely on local resources. We need the Spirit of Jesus to spark our imagination—the very Jesus who empowered a little boy with his loaves and fishes to feed a multitude.

10

FROM TEACHER (INSIDER)
TO GUIDE (OUTSIDER)

You cannot teach a man anything. You can
only help him to find it within himself.

GALILEO GALILEI

WHEN THE DAY FINALLY ARRIVED for the grand opening of Shalom Valley, I had recently passed the five-year mark of being cancer-free. I celebrated by applying for health insurance, which had been denied to me during those years because of my preexisting cancer condition. Little did the insurers know that I had really only sensed God inviting me to imagine five more years of life. Having passed that five-year window, I held life with more gratitude and fragility.

We had invited a few hundred Alongsiders to this opening camp, and they each gave a small financial contribution to cover the cost for their "little brothers and sisters" to attend. Phearom's stepsister, Srepo, who had been healed of demon possession and eventually became an Alongsider, would be there with her little sister. So many Alongsiders had signed up to bring their little brothers and sisters to camp that we eventually had to schedule three camps in a row to accommodate them all.

The Shalom Valley team stood nervously scanning the horizon as they waited for the buses to arrive. Some of the kids were coming from the other side of the country, and we knew that they would be arriving exhausted and carsick, but excited. Many of them had never been out of their province or seen the ocean before. I looked over at Chenda, who had helped with our community table during the pandemic lockdown, as she rushed around making last-minute arrangements.

Suddenly Phearom pointed and shouted, "Here they come!" A buzz of anticipation swept through the team of staff and volunteers as we formed two lines to welcome the kids off the bus with the traditional Khmer greeting, pressing our hands together at chest level in a posture of welcome and blessing.

The bus pulled into the driveway, and the mechanical door swung slowly ajar, but before it was fully open, the occupants were already squeezing out, taking in all the sights with wide eyes and tired exhilaration. Rising up in front of the campers was a huge, open-air meeting space. To the left, an industrial kitchen was being readied to provide meals for hundreds of children and youth.

The campers lugged their meager possessions up to the dormitories, beautiful earth-green, two-story buildings with new bunk beds that could sleep a hundred people in total. The girls found their rooms on the upper floor, and the boys fought over their preferred bunk beds on the ground floor.

The children ran from room to room, exploring. The first completely off-grid camp in the world, Shalom Valley had two wells to supply water and solar panels on the roofs of the dormitories to provide electricity.[1] Mart-Jan had devised a simple but effective onsite waste-treatment system to sanitize all the sewage so it could be released into the public drains. The whole camp was an engineering marvel.

Pon, who had worked alongside my dad in the early days clearing the ground under the hot sun, was proud of all that his construction crew had accomplished, and his eyes shone. While we still didn't have all the necessary official papers, there was little the government could do to stop us now that the construction had been completed.

As Chenda gathered the group of campers for an orientation, I sat back and marveled at how little I had to do. The Shalom Valley team would be running the whole camp from start to finish—and everything in between! The final hope of all who seek to be change makers is that others will take up the mantle and carry the vision forward themselves, and I was overjoyed as I watched the Shalom Valley team carry the mantle with such energy and enthusiasm.

The final gifting in the fivefold ministries outlined in Ephesians is the calling to teach. Those who seek to teach as outsiders in a crosscultural context must not simply transfer knowledge but must empower those who are insiders within the culture. Only then can they discover solutions themselves and work toward healing and transformation in ways that honor and engage the local knowledge and traditional values.

As outsiders, we must not remain teachers forever because, if we do, we ironically fail our calling. Thus, if we are going to nurture transformation in the world, we need to move beyond teaching and become humble guides instead.

TEACHER AS GUIDE

Paulo Freire, the renowned Brazilian philosopher and activist, sported thick glasses to correct his poor eyesight, wore his white hair combed back, and had a bushy, graying beard. He was born in 1921, grew up poor, and struggled to focus on his lessons at school. "I didn't understand anything because of my hunger," he lamented. "I wasn't dumb. It wasn't lack of interest. My social condition didn't allow me to have an education."[2]

This experience of poverty and exclusion influenced his decision to dedicate his life to improving the lives of the poor through radical education. Freire did not believe that the educational process could be neutral. Rather, education would either maintain the status quo and churn out more robots for the workforce, or it would become a guided "practice of freedom," the means by which people could grapple with reality and figure out how to be part of transforming the world.

Freire observed that most teaching is based on the "banking concept" of education, in which students are like empty bank accounts, subject to a series of deposits (or downloads) from the teacher. In such a system, the students are passive recipients of the information that is downloaded into them in the classroom. Many teachers expect their students to memorize and recall the information that they provide as expert instructors. There's no real participation, and the world is presented as static and unchangeable. You either give in or give up, making whatever adjustments are necessary to fit into the status quo. Freire saw such education as a system of oppression and control.

Freire wasn't interested in maintaining the status quo; he wished to upend it, so he advocated a "problem posing" method of education. In this approach, the teacher acts as a guide who helps students grapple with the truth—no matter how ugly— and frame it as a problem to be solved. The instructor exposes his or her own lack of knowledge instead of pretending to be an expert with all the answers. To engage the problem, students and teachers enter into a dialogue that will help them discover a solution together. The outsider-guide needs to come into a foreign context and help locals identify the problems they face rather than arriving as an expert teacher who downloads information.

▼ THE GUIDE ◢

Guides are gifted teachers who not only understand and explain truth but guide local people to discover the truth for themselves. Guides communicate God's wisdom in all kinds of ways as they help local people discern God's will. Rather than offering prepackaged answers, guides creatively help people work together to discover solutions for themselves.

As I watched Chenda leading the orientation at the first Shalom Valley camp, I remembered the day that I first saw her at an Alongsiders gathering, when she was around fifteen years old and in her fifth year as a "little sister." At the end of the gathering, she got up and told the group she had something to share, something she had discovered through her own experience. "I'm a little sister," Chenda began tentatively. "I lost my parents like many of you . . ." Her voice trailed off as she choked back tears.

Summoning strength from deep within, she looked up at the group and said boldly, "An Alongsider made all the difference in my life. I don't know where I would be if she hadn't come alongside me." Then with fiery passion, she said, "But listen to me, all of you. This takes commitment. You can't take on a little sister or brother and not visit them regularly! It would be better not to be an Alongsider than to be a flaky one!"

She stared around the room with fire in her eyes, as if daring anyone to disagree. I looked over at Nay and exchanged a grin. More than anything else, we knew that Alongsiders mentors were called to be guides themselves, helping their little brothers or sisters face the day-to-day challenges of life. Because Alongsiders mentors were young and untrained, they didn't come with ready-made answers. Instead, they committed to offer their compassionate presence as their little brothers or sisters faced problems.

Chenda continued, "I want to challenge every one of you right now to make that commitment to your little brother or sister. This is serious. This is someone's life!" The whole room was transfixed by Chenda's imposing presence, though she was barely five feet tall.

After that speech, I sought out Chenda and invited her to share more of her story, which she did with passion. Soon, she became an Alongsider herself, then a leader in the nationwide Alongsiders movement, and then the coordinator for this Shalom Valley camp week. Chenda fully owned the vision for Alongsiders because an Alongsider had made a huge difference in her own life.

The Alongsiders leadership team had already developed a model of group learning that seeks to empower youth to have a sense of ownership for the movement, centering the youth themselves rather than the teacher. We call this the OWNED learning ethos because we hope that Alongsiders will own both the problems they are facing with their little brothers and sisters and any possible solutions. The following explanation of the acronym sketches an overview of this OWNED model for learning.[3]

Observe the problem. This first step helps young people see the issues that they or their little brothers or sisters are facing. What the eye hasn't seen, the heart cannot grieve, so this first posture is an invitation to observe the problem and seek to understand it.

Weep over your own situation. The second step is ignored in most learning contexts, but it helps people carry the problem from their heads to their hearts. By lamenting a problem in our own lives and the lives of our loved ones, we make it personal and entertain the possibility that we could become wounded healers. Without a heartfelt, personal response we will not be truly motivated to make changes.

Narrow down root causes. In the third step, the group grapples with the root causes of the problem. Drawing a "problem tree" together can help the group identify the symptoms (leaves/fruit) of deeper issues (the roots of the tree). We must heal and nourish the roots to see any lasting change.

Explore solutions. Once the problem has been deconstructed, the group begins to explore possible solutions. Because the learners in the group own these ideas, they are much more likely to follow through on the necessary changes. In a typical classroom setting, a teacher usually skips from talking about the problem to telling the class about the solutions, without doing the important work of making it personal, being vulnerable, getting to the root issues, and giving the students space to imagine their own solutions. This approach undermines change because the solutions come from a distant expert instead of from those who are affected by the problem.

Decide on action. Finally, the group works together to formulate a plan and agree together on the actions that they will take. Knowledge without action leads nowhere (Jas 2:14), so the emphasis is on working together to enact change.

KINTSUGI: BEAUTY FROM BROKENNESS

After the orientation at that first Shalom Valley camp, the campers dispersed to various places for afternoon programming. I wandered upstairs to the open-air balcony, where Serey, who had trained Chenda to become an Alongsider, was leading a craft activity for the mentors. Serey was also a skilled and thoughtful guide.

I lowered myself onto the polished concrete floor and watched as the group spent the next forty-five minutes carefully painting and decorating small orange clay pots. The youth were buzzing about what they were making and what they would do with their pottery.

"I'm going to give this to my grandma. She'll like it."

"I'm going to give mine to my little sister for her birthday."

After the pottery decoration was finished, Serey held up her hand for silence. Then she quietly said, "I'm going to ask you to do something very hard now, but I want you to trust me. God has a lesson here for us, but you'll need to follow instructions, okay?"

There was a murmur of assent.

"I want you to take your clay pot and smash it on the concrete."

A jolt of shock went around the group, and everyone started to complain, "No! After all the work we put into this? Come on!"

"Trust me. There is a lesson in this for us."

One by one, the Alongsiders took their clay pots and tentatively broke them on the ground. There were sighs of resignation and a few pouty lips as they reluctantly smashed their beloved creations. I watched intently, somewhat shocked as I wondered what Serey was thinking. A part of me worried that we should have talked more about the kinds of workshop activities that would be appropriate with the Alongsiders. But I had been learning over the past years that I could trust Serey, so I checked myself.

When everyone had finished breaking their pots, Serey continued, "Okay, now that you have broken your clay pot, I want you to pick up the pieces one by one and place them in your hand. Look at them. These pieces represent the brokenness in your life—the failures, the ways your life hasn't turned out as you wanted. These pieces represent you, the real you."

I was holding back tears. I hadn't expected her lesson to apply to me.

The youth began to gather up the pieces carefully and cradle them in their hands. There was complete silence as a spirit of prayerfulness descended over the group. Through this object lesson, Serey had deftly helped the group move from observation to lament, which made their situation deeply personal.

Then Serey said, "Now take this glue and try to put your clay pot back together. As you do, invite God to show you how he puts together our broken pieces with love and care." Serey handed around the glue, and the Alongsiders concentrated on the task. One or two began to weep as the magnitude of God's loving care in the midst of their brokenness began to sink into their hearts.

After about twenty minutes, Serey asked the group if anyone would like to share. One of the girls immediately raised her hand. In a soft voice, she said, "My parents both died when I was a young girl. It broke me in pieces like this pot. I always looked at other kids with their parents and asked myself, *Why do they have someone to call Mama? Why do they have someone to call Papa, when I have no one?* I sobbed myself to sleep almost every night for months."

She looked around the group, and I knew that many of the other Alongsiders had experienced similar losses. They were also exploring the root causes of their brokenness. She continued, "But then God welcomed me into a church family, and the people in my church became my parents, my family. God was slowly putting me back together again. Without God's love in my life, I would still be broken. I would be nothing."

As tears streamed down her cheeks, her eyes shone with passion. "Later, I heard about Alongsiders, and I knew that God was giving me a chance to reach out to someone who had been through something similar. I chose my little sister because she had lost her mother too. I've been trying to love her and care for her because I know exactly what she is feeling."

I choked back emotion as Mart-Jan slid in beside me and put his hand on my back. Then Serey held up a laminated photo of some delicate Japanese pottery. "In Japan, there is an ancient art form called *Kintsugi*, which means 'golden repair.' They take broken pottery and repair it with gold powder. The final piece of *Kintsugi* is even more beautiful than the original."

She looked around the group. "That is what God is doing for you. He is taking your brokenness and remaking you to become even more beautiful than before. Your brokenness is still there and will always be part of who you are, but it has been transformed by God's touch. You are *Kintsugi*." A few of the Alongsiders sobbed as Serey spoke this word, *Kintsugi*, over them.

As I reflected on my own journey, I was amazed by this beautiful image for understanding God's plan for our lives as wounded healers and guides. There had been so many mistakes, hurts, and brokenness in my life. Many of the projects I had pioneered had faltered and died. I had invented creative new ways to mess up ministries and be a white savior. I had almost died of cancer, had struggled with other health and anxiety issues, and had spent almost two decades trying to serve God and change the world, but I still had more questions than answers.

Maybe God wanted to keep all these failures as a part of me. Maybe they weren't just missteps to brush away. Maybe they were part of my story—part of the story that God was writing in and through me in the world. Knowing I still had a lot to learn, I was deeply grateful to sit under Serey's gentle guidance.

SMALL BUT MIGHTY

On the final night of that first camp at Shalom Valley, we gathered for an extended time of singing, sharing, and praying under the night sky. The Alongsiders brought their repaired clay pots to show their little brothers and sisters, and we lifted our voices to God in song.

Phearom and Chenda led the closing program, but they asked me to share a few words of encouragement at the end. Speaking in Khmer, I shared from my heart, hoping that all the Alongsiders and their little brothers and sisters would discover something within themselves that was already there.

"In Cambodia, we have a famous proverb: 'Small but . . . ?'"

The young people finished the well-known proverb for me: ". . . mighty!"

"That's right. 'Small but mighty . . .'"

". . . weak but strong," they responded in unison.

"This proverb reflects the heart of how God works in the world. We all know the world looks down on those who are small and weak, poor and vulnerable, saying you are powerless and have nothing to offer. The people in charge say that you can't change the world because you need rich and powerful foreigners to bring about change and save the world for you." I choked back tears. "But they are wrong, for God says, 'I have chosen the weak things of this world to shame the powerful. I have chosen the lowly and downtrodden things of this world to shame the wise.'"[4]

I looked out at the faces of all the Alongsiders and their little brothers and sisters, which were illuminated by the lights in the open-air shelter. "I believe these things are coming true today in this very place.'" Then I handed Phearom the microphone and sat down.

Phearom continued, "God's ways are not the world's ways. God wants to use you to change the world—and you can start by small acts of faithfulness. You can faithfully walk alongside your little brother or sister day after day, week after week, year after year. Those small acts of commitment and faithfulness will be mighty when they are added together. Small but . . ."

"Mighty!" the kids yelled.

Then Phearom walked over and switched off the overhead lights. It was a cloudy, overcast night, and there were no stars lighting up the sky, so it suddenly got really dark. You could feel the atmosphere building with rain and storms. Though the shelter was covered with a huge roof, there were no walls, so we were partially exposed to the elements.

"We live in dark times," Phearom continued as the wind began to stir. "Our communities are filled with violence. Our leaders are violent. Some of your parents or other family members are struggling. Some use alcohol to forget their problems. Some use drugs. It is hard to see any light sometimes, and it's tough to have hope because so much brokenness is all around us."

Immersed in darkness, the group remained silent. Then Chenda walked over to a teenager on the edge of the group. Volunteers had already passed out unlit candles in paper cups to the Alongsiders and their little brothers and sisters. Chenda lit her candle with a lighter, and a tiny but bright flare burst into the darkness. Then she bent down and used her candle to light the candle of an Alongsider. "It only takes one person to bear the light and love of God to another," she said. "God wants each of you to bear light and bring change into the world."

Then the youth bent his candle toward his little brother's candle, and the light passed from him to another and another. As the light spread from one camper to another, the whole space began to light up, warmly illuminating each face. Someone began to sing, then others joined in, and as we sang, a mighty wind blew across Shalom Valley. As the wind lifted the dust from the ground and swirled around our legs, we sheltered our flickering candles in the paper cups, our shirts flapping and our hair blowing in our faces.

▲ ▼ ▲

I believe that a fresh wind is also blowing across the world today as God anoints those whom we least expect in the places where we least expect to find God, raising up the overlooked, downtrodden, oppressed, and marginalized.

God is graciously inviting "experts," who may even be acclaimed, successful, powerful, and accustomed to the limelight, to be caught up in this fresh wind as humble guides. But these outsiders are not central to the story God is writing in these places because local people will always be at the heart of what God is doing in each community. All who are ready to embrace this position of humility and wonder are welcome to join the movement, which is rising up all around the world.

11

DANGER #5
INDIVIDUALISM

The pursuit of full humanity cannot be carried out in isolation
or individualism, but only in fellowship and solidarity.

PAULO FREIRE

SHALOM VALLEY WAS FINALLY UP AND RUNNING as a social enterprise, but to make sure that it would turn a profit (or at least break even), we formed a Cambodian and Western management committee to support Phearom in his leadership role. We knew we would need a lot of technical input in order to run a business of this magnitude. But from the very beginning, these management meetings were hard going. The Westerners were used to robust debate in a business-meeting context and did not hold back from sharing their opinions. There was nothing nasty about it—no fistfights, headlocks, or mud wrestling—just simple disagreements about how to proceed, and we were used to grappling with challenges through lively debate.

The Cambodians found this approach uncomfortable. Through each meeting, they sat quietly, hesitant to offer their opinions at all. It was easy to slip into a pattern where the Westerners dominated the decision making, which was the complete opposite of our hopes and intentions.

To give the Cambodians an upper hand in communicating, I suggested that we conduct all our meetings in Khmer language. This forced the Westerners, who all spoke Khmer, to listen more carefully and to limit their speaking. Insisting on speaking English in a non-English context is one of the ways that benevolent outsiders hold onto their power and privilege because they will always maintain the dominant hand in communications. That's why learning to communicate in the local language is such an important part of laying down our privilege.

This decision certainly helped put us on more equal footing, but I continued to wonder what was beneath our vastly different approaches to communication. After some in-depth reading and research, I gathered the management committee together to look at *The Geography of Thought* by the social psychologist Richard Nisbett.[1] I felt his perspective might provide us with some helpful insights.

As we sat on a fishing platform in the middle of the pond at Shalom Valley, a gentle breeze kept blowing my handouts as I passed them around. Trying to summarize Nisbett's argument, I explained that there is an underlying worldview in Cambodia and across Asia that flows from deep cultural roots in China, which is totally different from the Western way of seeing the world that flows from ancient Greece.

The group looked at the handout, and I could see they were struggling to follow my summary. I abandoned my papers and tried a story. "Basically, the geography of China—flat fertile plains—lent itself really well to the cultivation of rice, and so steaming white rice became the staple diet of much of Asia." Phearom, Pon, and Marea nodded their heads. "So three times a day, you eat rice, right? As you often say, 'If you haven't eaten rice, you haven't eaten.'"

"That's true!" They all laughed.

Next, I contrasted China's geography with Greece's, which was more lush and mountainous, so hunting, fishing, and trading along the coastline became the primary means of putting food on the table each night. "In Greece," I explained, "they didn't even develop agriculture until two thousand years after China."

I went on to describe how in China growing rice as a staple meant that local people had to band together to build irrigation systems. "You had to work with your neighbors or you would starve, and if you got on the wrong side of the village head honcho—watch out, he might cut off your water supply and you'd be in BIG trouble." Again, I could see Phearom, Pon, and Marea nodding in agreement, but the Westerners leaned forward, seeking understanding.

"In China, each person was first and foremost a member of a group or several collectives—the clan, the village, and the family," I continued. "From this communal way of life flowed the powerful organizing principle of harmony." Once again Phearom, Pon, and Marea nodded. "So, in most of Asia, social harmony was not just the highest pursuit but the key to survival. No harmony, no rice. No rice, you die."

"Yes!" Marea exclaimed. "That's what my grandmother says!"

"Meanwhile, over in the Mediterranean," I continued, "the Greeks were able to find food and support their families by themselves. They didn't really need to work together with neighbors or worry about getting on the wrong side of Uncle Aesop down the lane. The Greeks, more than any other ancient peoples, had a remarkable sense of personal agency—the sense that they were in charge of their own lives and completely free to act however they chose. Does that sound like anyone you know?"

This time the Westerners began to nod. Once these insights started to make sense to the whole group, we began to discuss how the Greeks organized their society around democratic assemblies in cities, where decisions were made by rigorous debate, logical arguments, and rhetoric. There was no need to worry about offending anyone else because no one held anyone's livelihood in their hands. Everyone was free to speak out and pursue whatever they thought was right.

"From this individualistic way of life flowed the powerful organizing principle of liberty," I continued. "For many white Westerners, liberty, individual freedom, and self-expression are the highest pursuits. 'You do you!' And this value for self-expression and liberty flowed into every Western nation—from Europe to North America to my country, New Zealand, and beyond."

This insight generated a lively discussion about how a lot of Westerners[2] see themselves as the main heroes in a movie about themselves whereas a lot of Easterners see themselves as supporting cast members, part of a greater whole, where no one acts alone. We further observed how Westerners have rights whereas Easterners have obligations.

"The Eastern worldview, which is based on harmony," I added, "has a much clearer picture of the interrelatedness of all things. Every action a person takes impacts a lot of other people."

We talked about how the Eastern worldview (based on harmony) understands context whereas the Western worldview (based on liberty) encourages each person to carve his or her own way through life in order to find freedom and happiness. "Because there is not as much of a need to calculate the impact that our decisions will have on anyone else, the Western worldview is deeply individualistic," I concluded. Then we discussed how these worldviews related to every aspect of life—from child rearing to decision making to personal finances.

"The ancient Greeks fine-tuned their debating skills into an art form in their schools for philosophy," I observed. "They developed logic and a linear way of thinking that has borne heaps of fruit in the sciences and technology."

I compared this approach with the ancient Chinese, who viewed the world in a more circular and interconnected way. "They dedicated themselves to art and poetry, so they developed a deeper sense of paradox, an ability to hold two opposing truths in tension." I gathered up all my handouts so they wouldn't blow into the water and shrugged. "So, you can imagine how these different skills and perspectives might play themselves out in our management meetings, right?"

The group began to buzz as we all talked about why the Westerners were speaking up more often and more insistently, using debating skills that had been developed and encouraged from an early age. But we could also see how we were riding roughshod over the Cambodians, who were more concerned about maintaining harmony.

The Cambodians said that they felt we sometimes communicated in ways that bordered on being rude, which threatened the harmony of the group. Moreover, they felt we often couldn't see the bigger picture of community connectedness that was so important to them.

Then Phearom spoke up. "Craig, remember when Shalom Valley was getting overrun by half a dozen wild dogs, and they kept stealing our shoes, and then one time they bit someone?" I nodded and leaned forward, remembering how Phearom and I had butted heads about those diseased dogs time and time again. I had gotten more upset every time I visited Shalom Valley and saw the dogs there, snarling and growling, because I considered them to be a menace and potential danger for campers. I had even threatened to deal with them myself on multiple occasions. The Cambodians had just laughed nervously and ignored me—even when I offered them ten dollars a head for any dogs they could catch and dispose of.

Phearom continued, "Well, we knew that if we killed those wild dogs, we would upset the owner, who was a neighbor, and we knew that if we upset this owner, it would cause us a lot of problems further down the track in the village. So I talked to the owner and asked him to come pick them up, but I had to keep phoning and politely reminding him, week after week. That's why we couldn't get rid of them quickly. But you were so upset, so I didn't say anything." He chuckled.

"So was the owner that guy who turned up with a sack?"

Phearom nodded and laughed again. I could see how his high value for harmony had clashed with my high value for individual liberty and quick results. By now, I'd been living in Cambodia more than a decade, but these cultural insights were still only slowly moving from my head to my heart.

My experience with the wild dogs at Shalom Valley shed light on the danger of individualism for outsiders. As I reflected on our conversation as a management team, I began to realize how my individualistic Western worldview had affected my understanding of the gospel. When I was growing up, the gospel was presented to me as my *personal* response to God. *I* had sinned, and *I* was guilty of a spiritual crime that deserved to be punished by God. This made perfect sense to me in my Western context of New Zealand, where I was expected to trust the justice system and I was completely free to make my own decisions about faith independently of my family or anyone else. In fact, we were encouraged to keep our religious convictions private and personal.

But in Cambodia and other Eastern contexts, the shame of letting down family or not doing one's duty is a more real, everyday experience than any feeling of private, personal guilt. Most Cambodians don't trust the justice system in their country. After all, a guilty verdict is directly correlated to how much cash you slip under the table to the judge. So petty thieves and drunk drivers are routinely beaten by mobs, who are convinced that they won't see justice otherwise. I once stopped a group of neighbors from attacking a local boy whom they caught stealing. Obviously, most Cambodians would interpret terms such as *guilty, innocent, law, punishment,* and *divine justice* very differently from the way most Westerners do.

SEEING THE GOSPEL WITH NEW EYES

A few days after our conversation on the fishing platform at Shalom Valley, I had to travel to India for an Alongsiders meeting, and I found myself in a meeting room in Chennai with my mentor, Paulus. When I asked Paulus some of these questions, his dark, wise eyes crinkled with his trademark smile. He said softly, "Here in this part of the world, we are a people who understand family and community. We understand honor and shame. And we understand hospitality and feasting. All these things are in the Gospels—you just have to have eyes to see them."

He reached for his worn Bible, flicked to Luke 15, and ran his leathery finger down the page until he got to the parable of the prodigal son. "In this story, you have a boy who dishonors his father by asking for the inheritance before he dies, demanding that his father sell half of the very farm he is standing on. His actions are like a curse on his father—as if he is wishing that his father would die, the very man he is supposed to honor and respect more than anyone."

Paulus shook his head sadly. "This kind of thing would be deeply offensive for our people. This son is bringing shame on his father, on his whole family. His father should disown him there and then. He should banish him, but instead the father takes the shame on himself by giving the boy his inheritance." Paulus paused, then looked at me and smiled. "Amazing, eh?"

He sighed and then continued. "The boy goes off proudly and selfishly to make his way in the world, without giving any thought to his family or the needs of his community. More shame! More dishonor! And then he ends up in trouble and has to work with the pigs." Paulus looked closely at me and lowered his voice. "That kind of work would be very humiliating for the Jews—and also for the Muslim people here in India. The son has lost all his dignity by this point. What a sad, sad journey, eh?"

Paulus closed his eyes as he reflected on this sad moment in the story. Then he took a deep breath. "Finally, the boy decides to go home. His head is hanging with shame, and he is covered in pig filth, wearing ragged clothes. Now everyone knows that when you return home after going away, you need to arrive as a success—a man who made it in the city. You're supposed to be a big deal now, right?"

Paulus laughed. "I'm sure it's the same in Cambodia as it is in India. You come home from the city, bearing presents for everyone, and everyone is happy. To come back empty handed and destitute is a humiliating sign of failure. Again, this son should be rejected by his father. But once again, the father chooses not to reject and shame his son. In fact, the father runs into the street to meet his impoverished son in a very undignified manner!"

Paulus's dark eyes widened in amazement. "We could not imagine such hospitality and forgiveness here in India! This father takes his son's shame on himself by welcoming him back into the family." He thumped the Bible shut. "This amazing welcome is what God offers to all of us—and then the story ends with a big feast! You see, it's a very Asian story, eh, Craig?"

Reading the Scripture through Asian eyes, I felt like I was seeing God the Father in a new light. Reading this parable as a shocking story about family and community, honor and shame, poverty and feasting made so much more sense to me than recounting the gospel as a formula with four "spiritual laws." I imagined that the gospel illuminated by this parable would make complete sense to Cambodians, as such stories reflect their heart language of harmony and community.

As I continued to reflect on Paulus's retelling of this parable, I sensed God inviting me to go even deeper. As I opened my heart to the story, I sensed God speaking into my soul:

This is my love story for you, too, Craig. I've been waiting a long time for you to listen. It is the good news you need to hear right now. But do you have ears to hear what I am saying to you? Like the prodigal son, you, too, have wanted to go out into the world. You, too, have been driven to make a difference, to make your mark, to return home with honor and esteem.

You are worried about failure. You are worried about being shamed. You are worried about what other people might think, how they might label you. You are worried about so many things.

But whether you achieve your goals, or not, whether you change the world, or not, my love for you does not change. In the story, the son's success or failure in the big city made no difference to his father's love for him. Either way, the father would have run toward him with open arms. Either way, that boy would always be a welcome part of the family. He would always be loved.

Wherever you go, you will be my son. Wherever you go, you will be my beloved. Wherever you go, you will always be welcomed home, into a community of people, and your inheritance will be yours. There is nothing you can do to earn that inheritance. You are my beloved son, in whom I am well pleased.

I shut my eyes and wept as I felt the Father's healing love flood my soul. Would I be a world-changer? Perhaps. Or perhaps not. Certainly not as a lone ranger.

Would I always be a beloved child of God? Yes! Yes, I would.

EPILOGUE

*That's why you go to the margins. Not to make
a difference, but that they can guide you.*

FATHER GREGORY BOYLE

FOR THREE MONTHS, Shalom Valley has been booked solid, and the enterprise is almost breaking even as a result of renting the venue to other groups when the Alongsiders movement isn't using it. Busloads of enthusiastic kids have arrived week after week, full of excitement and ready to play and learn in a safe environment. They wolf down the nutritious meals three times a day, loading up their plates with outrageous amounts of rice as well as seafood from the local fishermen.

Local Khmer churches have finally found a place where they can afford to gather for church camps. Schools and NGOs working with children have had a blast with confidence-building games on the obstacle course. And, of course, the youth love all the adventure and fun they have during camp.

I am visiting Shalom Valley for a week of camp that was booked especially for a local school built for children in a slum-relocation site. Most of these kids have never been out of their own province or seen the ocean, so they are full of wonder and joy. As I watch them sing, dance, and laugh, I know that some may shed tears when they have to leave.

In Phearom's trademark understated way, he is modeling strong and gentle leadership to the talented young Cambodians from the school, who are eager to become leaders themselves.

I smile when I see Kevin, my old friend from Vancouver, who is sitting in the back row of the open-air pavilion, nodding his head with the beat of the worship music. I walk over and put my hand on his shoulder, and he gives me a broad smile.

After overcoming his addiction, Kevin moved to Cambodia and into the slum-relocation site, where he worked with the local community to establish a school. Though his journey has been painful, God has worked through him to strengthen local Cambodian leaders who have caught a vision of hope for the restoration of their community.

The mantra, "Cook too much food, invite too many people," could well be the slogan for Shalom Valley camp, just as it was when Kevin lived with our family in Vancouver. But it's also a picture of the kingdom of God reigning here on earth. God's global feast is abundant and open to all. We are all invited to the table to partake in the feast and to contribute something to the potluck. Kevin reminds me that God works through the most unlikely people, and his presence at Shalom Valley gives me hope that God is calling everyone to join the feast.

Discerning Your Vision for the Future

Throughout this book, I hope you have taken time to reflect on your missional type within your own service context. I hope you are energized by these five new ways of engaging with today's world and are ready to address the key areas we overlook as outsiders (power, complicity, secularism, money, and individualism) so that together we can find a better and more beautiful vision for how we can bear the light of God's love into the world—serving in a new era.

If you sense that you have received an apostolic gifting, God may be calling you as an outsider to serve as a *catalyst*, who will partner with local insiders to spearhead tangible works of service (*diakonia*) that will benefit the poor and needy, and build up the body of Christ. The outsider catalyst is an innovative and self-disciplined entrepreneur who creatively perseveres in the task of working with local leaders to bring about change within the systems and powers of the world. In the new era, catalysts will serve as social entrepreneurs, NGO cofounders, and visionaries as they imitate the spirit of humility and servanthood that Jesus models.

If you sense that you have received a prophetic gifting, God may be calling you as an outsider to serve as an *ally*, who will stand alongside the marginalized around the world to help amplify their voices. The outsider ally will use his or her privilege and power to come alongside those who are oppressed and to promote the liberty of those who don't have the same freedoms by speaking truth to power. In the new era, allies will serve as journalists, bloggers, activists, holy troublemakers, protestors, artists, and creative thinkers as they imitate the spirit of courage and wisdom that Jesus embodies.

If you sense that you have received an evangelistic gifting, God may be calling you as an outsider to serve as a *seeker*, who will slowly and deeply learn the culture and language of the place where you live. The outsider seeker will look for redemptive analogies and cultural touchpoints so that those who have never heard about God's vision of shalom can discover what it means to worship Jesus in a culturally meaningful way. In the new era, seekers will serve as anthropologists, linguists, retreat facilitators, preachers, and conversationalists as they engage others with a spirit of appreciative inquiry and seek to learn before talking. Seekers will model their engagement with others on Jesus, who asked over three hundred questions and answered only three.

If you sense that you have received a pastoral gifting, God may be calling you as an outsider to serve as a *midwife*, who will help local people birth communities of faith that are both contextual and replicable, particularly among the poorest and least-resourced communities in the world. The outsider midwife will follow the example of Jesus, who promised that, first and foremost, his gospel would be "good news to the poor" (Lk 4:18). In the new era, midwives will serve as pastoral trainers, counselors, shadow church planters, spiritual formation practitioners, and servant leaders as they empower and strengthen the hands of others. Midwives will model their engagement with others on Jesus, who came to serve rather than be served.

If you sense that you have received a gift of teaching, God may be calling you as an outsider to serve as a *guide*, who will come alongside others and empower them to envision change and healing within their communities. In this way, the vital work of transformation will be led by local people, who will implement local ideas that rely on local resources and are fully owned. In the new era, guides will serve as teachers, trainers, coaches, professors, and laborers from every other trade and profession under the sun as they equip those who can envision their communities being healed and restored. Guides will model their engagement with others on Jesus, who didn't stay on earth forever but walked alongside his team of disciples and then empowered *them* to go out and do likewise.

This new wave of global servants may not be called missionaries, and they will definitely not fit the old molds and models of missionary work. In today's pluralistic global setting, we need fresh metaphors to frame our new ways of thinking and being in the world, so let us describe these outsider servants as catalysts, allies, seekers, midwives, and guides.

Finally, all who leave their passport country to serve God in crosscultural contexts will need to do the deep and ongoing work of dealing with their cultural baggage. All who come from the west, the east, the north, and the south, and every place of power and privilege, must repent of the ways we have collectively exported our sins and biases throughout history and continue to do so in our present age.

Let us lay down our posture of dominance, especially when we are working with the poor and marginalized, and embrace vulnerability and open-handedness instead.

Let us repent of our complicity in the historical sins of our nations through colonialism, militarism, injustice, materialism, and exploitation—and promote justice, reconciliation, and creative nonviolence instead.

Let us confess our secular ways of thinking and seek to learn from those who see the world in more holistic ways. Let us also become more aware of our individualistic worldviews and seek to learn from those who see interconnectedness and harmony within God's creation.

As Jesus taught us, it is only by dying to ourselves that we will find life (Mk 8:35). None of us know if we will have five months, five years, or five decades more to walk this earth. But Jesus invites us to follow him along the pathway of vulnerability and uncertainty, for out of our brokenness and fragility, God will reform each of us into the beloved people he created us to be in the world.

Go and serve humbly alongside—in submission to God and local leaders. Jesus sends you out.

The End Is the Beginning

As Kevin and I talk quietly while the children sing, he whispers that he and his family are preparing to move out of the slum community, where they have invested so many years.

"Outsiders always leave, eventually," I observe with a wry smile.

Kevin nods. "I know. I just hope some of the insiders who've become leaders will remain over the long haul. But that's out of my hands."

We both know that it is our privilege as outsiders to walk alongside the insiders we come to know for a time and to watch them catch a vision for the healing and transformation of their own communities. However long we might have this privilege to journey as alongsiders, we trust that God will continue to work in and through all of us—both insiders and outsiders—for the good of the whole world.

ACKNOWLEDGMENTS

I WISH I COULD INCLUDE THE NAMES and give due credit to every person who was part of how the events in this story unfolded, but that would be a different kind of book.

However, I would be remiss not to give credit to my parents, who were involved in the story from the very beginning—right from the first week we set aside to fast, pray, and listen to God about Cambodia's first adventure camp—what would, in time, become Shalom Valley. After twenty years of service in Singapore, when most people would be settling into retirement, my parents humbled themselves to work for their own son. My father and Pon worked side by side under the sweltering heat of the Cambodian sun as they physically cleared the land. Mum and Dad walked in the humble footsteps of my missionary grandparents in India before them, showing me how to serve in respectful and empowering ways.

Mart-Jan and Talitha van der Maas also played a key role in building Shalom Valley during the crucial construction phase. Mart-Jan's dedication to architectural quality is reflected throughout every building on the site. Today, he is back in Holland, birthing a European Alongsiders movement, and I couldn't be prouder of him. Phearom, Pon, Marea, Lakhina, Daroth, Paul, Alli, and numerous others have provided leadership and support over these crucial early years. Their hard work and sacrifice have borne much fruit and will do so for years to come.

Through all of this, my wife, Nay, has played a steadying role in my life and the wider ministry. She is a source of blessing, wisdom, and stability for me, our children, and so many others across multiple countries. Everyone who knows us quickly realizes that she is the warm and friendly one, who gets on and does the work, while I talk and write about it. For this, I am eternally grateful. Her contributions at Shalom Valley and as a cofounder and leader in Alongsiders are too numerous to mention.

OVERVIEW OF THE FIVE MISSIONAL TYPES

HOW DO WE BRIDGE THE DIVIDE between our cultures, gifts, and contexts so that we can serve alongside local people in a crosscultural setting? The first step is to know ourselves and explore more deeply who God has uniquely created us to be.

CATALYST (APOSTLE)

Catalysts are wired as entrepreneurs for the kingdom, not just the church. In their commitment to God's people around the world, they are self-disciplined and mature enough to say, not "my kingdom" but "your kingdom come," Lord (Mt 6:10). Catalysts refuse to build their own empires but seek to help spark something new in partnership with those insider apostles who will lead the movement going forward. By nature, they are future oriented and want to work with local people in new and uncharted contexts.

Here are some examples of catalysts: social entrepreneurs, investors, NGO cofounders, visionaries, innovators, dreamers, and networkers.

ALLY (PROPHET)

Allies know God's heart for the marginalized, so they seek to come alongside and use their privilege to amplify voices that are struggling to be heard. They care deeply about justice and mercy and are bold enough to speak truth to power in situations of injustice. As outsiders, they are uniquely positioned to question the status quo and call the global community toward God's kingdom on earth, using their privilege (access, training, and resources) to support the causes championed by local prophets.

Here are some examples of allies: activists, community organizers, journalists, bloggers, social media communicators, lawyers, videographers, reporters, documentarians, protestors, rebels, artists, and creative thinkers.

SEEKER (EVANGELIST)

Seekers search for redemptive analogies and cultural touchpoints as a way of bridging the universal truth of the gospel with local understanding. They are enthusiasts for contextualization, storytelling, and creativity. As outsiders, they arrive as students of language and culture and are more likely to ask questions than offer answers. They work with insider evangelists to understand and communicate what the kingdom of God looks like in each new context.

Here are some examples of seekers: translators, travelers, cultural anthropologists, linguists, historians, retreat leaders, preachers, communicators, and writers.

MIDWIFE (PASTOR)

Midwives are pastorally gifted leaders who nurture and protect the people of God, helping insider pastors/shepherds birth and care for communities of faith. As outsiders, they are passionate about cultivating the local church and developing disciples without needing to be in the limelight. They are careful to use church-planting approaches that can be replicated without outside resources.

Here are some examples of midwives: pastoral trainers, leadership developers, coaches, counselors, social workers, shadow church planters, spiritual formation practitioners, mentors, and servant leaders.

GUIDE (TEACHER)

Guides are gifted teachers who not only understand and explain truth but guide local people to discover the truth for themselves. Guides communicate God's wisdom in all kinds of ways as they help local people discern God's will. Rather than offering prepackaged answers, guides creatively help people work together to discover solutions for themselves.

Here are some examples of guides: teachers, theologians, trainers, community development practitioners, coaches, professors, and those who are passionate about solving problems and bringing healing.

DISCOVERING YOUR MISSIONAL TYPE

THE FOLLOWING QUICK AND SIMPLE QUESTIONNAIRE is designed to help you discern your vocational gifting as a catalyst, ally, seeker, midwife, or guide.

INSTRUCTIONS

Answer each question below with a rating of 1 to 10, depending on how well it applies to you. Score 1 if the statement does not apply to you at all and up to 10 if the statement is a good fit. Be bold in marking to the extremes. If you prefer, you can take this test online and receive extra resources for your journey. (Go to www.craiggreenfield.com/missionaltypes.)

1 = the statement does not apply at all → 10 = the statement is very accurate

____ I get angry at bullies and enjoy standing up to them whenever I can.

____ I like a "blank sheet of paper" and a chance to come up with new ideas.

____ I want people to experience the welcome of Christ in fellowship with others.

_____ People tell me I am good at communicating complex ideas in simple ways.

_____ I will often share my story with people I have just met.

_____ I have a history of taking vulnerable people under my wing and fighting for them.

_____ I see the big picture and emerging themes in the world—and I want to engage.

_____ I have a heart for the local church and want to see it thrive.

_____ I'm a reader—the Bible, books, articles, theories. I love learning.

_____ I am adaptable. From a mud hut to an international hotel, I can fit in.

_____ I don't mind making people angry if there's a good reason. I can be blunt.

_____ I have a history of starting new projects and recruiting people to help me.

_____ I have a history of supporting, equipping, and training young leaders.

_____ If I don't understand something, I will invest time to figure it out.

_____ I'm good at language learning.

_____ I want to help the oppressed. I cannot stand by as injustice occurs.

_____ I like rallying a group toward a common cause.

_____ I tend to focus more on the body of believers than on those outside the church.

_____ I love to help people solve complex problems step by step.

_____ I love to share and talk with people, even strangers.

_____ I see what is wrong with society, and I want to make it right.

_____ I'm not afraid to bend the rules or cut a few corners to make things happen.

_____ I love to see people come together to encourage each other.

_____ I share the new things God is teaching me with others.

_____ I love chatting with people from other religions.

To identify your dominant area of vocational gifting, enter your scores (1–10) for each question in the corresponding box below. (See table 1.) For example, the catalyst corresponds to questions 4, 9, 14, 19, and 24. Add up the individual scores for each type. This will give you an overall score for that type. A higher score indicates a stronger gifting in this area of ministry.

Table 1. Scoring the test for missional type

Missional Type	Enter your score beside each question number					Total
Catalyst	2	7	12	17	22	
Ally	1	6	11	16	21	
Seeker	5	10	15	20	25	
Midwife	3	8	13	18	23	
Guide	4	9	14	19	24	

You can also take this test online at www.craiggreenfield .com (www.craiggreenfield.com/missionaltypes). After completing the test, you will receive a free PDF with a more in-depth description of each vocational type.

QUESTIONS FOR REFLECTION AND DISCUSSION

THESE QUESTIONS CAN BE USED for individual reflection or group discussion. You may wish to go through the book discussing each chapter week by week or have a single whole-book discussion in which your group chooses just a handful of questions to cover.

PREFACE, INTRODUCTION, AND CHAPTER 1

1. A *Christianity Today* article laments, "For many, missions is a story of heroes and gospel advance. For others, missions is a story of colonialism, genocide, triumphalism, and cross-cultural disasters." Which of these sides do you find the most compelling? Why? Do you see yourself responding to this analysis with a fight, flight, or freeze response?

2. If you received a diagnosis that gave you only five more years to live, what would you do with those years?

3. Can you think of ways in which the fivefold ministry types of Ephesians 4:11 (apostle, prophet, evangelist, pastor, teacher) might not translate to a crosscultural context in

which you hold drastically more power and privilege than local people?

CHAPTER 2. CATALYST (INSIDER) OR APOSTLE (OUTSIDER)

1. What do you think about the statement, "No one enters the kingdom without a letter of reference from the poor"? What might this mean in your church, neighborhood, workplace, or school?

2. Read Acts 2:42-47. If you have ever experienced going to a camp, discuss how the experience echoed the way the earliest believers met together daily and shared all things in common. Are there other contexts where you have experienced the depth of community lived by the early followers of Christ?

CHAPTER 3. DANGER #1: POWER

1. Share some examples of ministries that you think do well in sharing both the "tragedy" and the "resilience" of the poor and marginalized.

2. Have you experienced any of the following traps? If so, share some examples:

   • The omniscience trap: assuming you know more than local people.

   • The omnipresence trap: staying around too long or engaging too often.

   • The omnipotence trap: solving people's problems for them instead of pointing them to God.

Chapter 4. Ally (Outsider) or Prophet (Insider)

1. Discuss some of the instances when Jesus spoke out against injustice. If Jesus spoke out against injustice, why do you think the church is often silent about injustice?

2. Here are some examples of Old Testament prophets speaking out against injustice.

   - "Hear this, you who trample the needy / and do away with the poor of the land" (Amos 8:4).

   - "Learn to do right; seek justice. / Defend the oppressed. / Take up the cause of the fatherless; / plead the case of the widow" (Is 1:17).

   - "Woe to him who builds his palace by unrighteousness, / his upper rooms by injustice" (Jer 22:13).

   - "Now this was the sin of your sister Sodom: She and her daughters were arrogant, overfed and unconcerned; they did not help the poor and needy" (Ezek 16:49).

   - "He has shown you, O mortal, what is good. / And what does the LORD require of you? / To act justly and to love mercy / and to walk humbly with your God" (Mic 6:8).

   - "This is what the LORD Almighty said: . . . Do not oppress the widow or the fatherless, the foreigner or the poor" (Zech 7:9-10).

Why do you think the role of the prophet is often understood as a personal "fortuneteller" in our churches rather than someone who rails against injustice?

3. Dietrich Bonhoeffer said, "Silence in the face of evil is itself evil: God will not hold us guiltless. Not to speak is

to speak. Not to act is to act." Is there a particular injustice that God has been stirring you to speak about lately?

CHAPTER 5. DANGER #2: COMPLICITY

1. Review the prayer of Daniel in Daniel 9:4-11 (political context + repentance). Why do you think repentance for our nation's sins is not widely taught?

2. What national sins might your country need to grapple with before God?

3. Shalom is God's answer to the question, "What should the world be like?" As you read Jeremiah 29:4-11, what aspects of shalom do you see?

4. How might God's vision for shalom guide our voting?

CHAPTER 6. SEEKER (OUTSIDER) OR EVANGELIST (INSIDER)

1. What do you think Catherine Doherty meant when she said, "We do not go to mission lands to bring Jesus Christ, as much as to uncover him where he already is"?

2. Jesus didn't repeat a formula or steps for salvation. Instead, he often spoke good news into a particular situation of bad news. Where do you see this happening in the Gospels? Where do you see this happening in your context?

3. How have you seen "bomb-crater theology" working in your own life and in the lives of your loved ones?

CHAPTER 7. DANGER #3: SECULARISM

1. Why do you think it is said that over the past two centuries "Western missionaries have been a major source of secularization throughout Asia and Africa"?

2. Craig gives examples of exorcisms and demon possession. Do you think these things still happen today? Why do we rarely see them in the West?

3. Shane Claiborne is quoted as saying, "We can only be Good Samaritans if we're willing to be close to the kind of streets where people get beat up." Put differently, we can only encounter marginalized people if we're willing to go to the margins. What might this mean for you?

CHAPTER 8. MIDWIFE (OUTSIDER) OR PASTOR (INSIDER)

1. Consider Craig's words about trust and control:

   We carry the baggage of privilege. This can include a lack of confidence in local people's ability to think and make decisions for themselves. Though it is often packed tightly into a hidden corner of a suitcase, this is the false savior mindset—a pattern of dominance. Though many of us truly want to see transformation, deep down we are tempted to believe that we must be the executors of that transformation. Instead of demonstrating the fruit of *self*-control, we seek to control others.

How have you seen evidence of this challenge in the ministries with which you have been involved?

2. Why do you think the role of pastor has become more similar to a CEO or executive director in our Western churches? Where have you seen the role of pastor practiced differently?

3. Craig uses the metaphor of a midwife to reimagine church planting in a crosscultural context. How does a midwife differ from a pastor?

CHAPTER 9. DANGER #4: MONEY

1. Craig shares the following four reasons why we need to be cautious about using outside money to achieve change in contexts of poverty.

   - The initiative may lack sustainability if the money runs out.

   - Money distorts the relationship between the wisdom of a project and the results.

   - Money concentrates power in the hands of donors instead of the poor and vulnerable.

   - Using money to drive change can't be easily replicated by local people.

Which of these do you find most compelling? Why?

2. What common church-planting practices result in locals being unable to replicate the church plant, and why is this such a problem?

Chapters 10. Guide (Outsider) or Teacher (Insider)

1. In your own educational experience, were you more exposed to what Paulo Freire describes as the "banking concept" of education or the "problem posing" method of education?

2. Share about times when you experienced the "problem posing" method. How did that affect you?

3. Which part of the OWNED framework resonates with you the most?

Chapter 11. Danger #5: Individualism

1. Craig describes the difference between the Western cultural foundation of liberty and the Eastern cultural foundation of harmony. Which of these foundations resonates more with your experience? Discuss examples of how you see these cultural differences playing out in your context (e.g., child rearing, family duty, career, opportunity to go into mission work, communication style, etc.).

2. Read the story of the prodigal son in Luke 15:11-32 and consider it within the light of an honor/shame culture. How might this affect how you share the gospel story in such a context?

Chapter 12. Appendixes and Inventory

1. Complete the missional type inventory in appendix 2.

2. Of the five missional types, which one (or two) resonates most deeply with you?

3. What is your biggest takeaway from this book?

ALONGSIDERS
INTERNATIONAL

IN MUCH OF THE WORLD, more than half of the population is less than twenty-five years old. Forty-nine of those countries are in Africa, and the rest are scattered throughout Asia, the Middle East, and Latin America. In the countries with the youngest population, the median age is just fifteen years old.

The vast majority of children and young people alive on earth today are living in economically poor families and communities that are far removed from the world's centers of wealth, power, and resources. These young people living at the margins are not a problem to solve or a burden to carry but rather a tremendous source of hope and capability. Rather than trying to fix the "problem" of so many young people at the margins, we can begin to partner with them as leaders and problem solvers. This partnership might usher in the shalom of God.

Business leaders and investors already recognize the immense potential of these young people as entrepreneurs, innovators, and consumers. The United Nations calls the youth of today "a new global power reshaping the world." They're also asking a good question, "What can we do to unleash the creativity and potential of the largest youth cohort humanity has ever seen?" Christians who believe in the gospel that Jesus proclaimed and want to live by his example need to be asking the same question.

ALONGSIDER MOVEMENTS

What if young Christians in thousands of local churches around the world embraced the call to love their neighbors and make disciples in their own communities? Those youth would make a simple but powerful commitment: to walk alongside one little brother or sister each. They would stir up their local churches and become bearers of the gospel in their own neighborhoods. As they grow in leadership, maturity, and integrity, others would follow their examples. Children and families would come to faith, and we could anticipate improved health and well-being for children, reductions in family violence and abuse, and increased cooperation between neighbors. Countless lives would be changed.

This may sound like a wildly speculative wish list, but it's based in reality. The first Alongsider movement began in Cambodia in 2003. Now, Alongsiders are being mobilized in a growing number of countries around the world. Every movement starts with a simple, profound vision: no child left behind. Every Christian youth can be a disciple maker. In other words, build a loving relationship with one vulnerable child from your own community and make a difference in his or her life.

Along with vulnerable children, the Alongsiders themselves are being transformed as they become disciples of Jesus while serving and making disciples among the next generation. This holistic process is unique for each Alongsider, but the following are some general impacts:

1. They choose a lifestyle of love and compassion for another human being.

2. They develop important life skills as they cooperate with each other, with other members of the local church, and with parents and leaders to overcome barriers and solve problems.

3. They practice servant leadership and receive valuable training along the way, becoming leaders who are known by their love.

4. They begin a pattern of relational disciple making that will last for the rest of their lives.

5. They find purpose and hope in being part of a movement that is changing lives in their church, community, and country.

The Khmer proverb, "It's easier to bend a tree when it's young," suggests that the patterns and values that we practice when we're young will last our entire lives. When young Christians become disciples of Jesus and disciple makers, they'll likely continue in the same pattern going forward. And, in time, they'll influence the direction and character of their local churches.

THE SUNDAY SCHOOL MOVEMENT

Over two hundred years ago, a young man in a forgotten corner of England surveyed the state of his society and became determined to respond. Robert Raike was walking down St. Catherine's Street in Gloucester when he spotted a little boy in a tattered blue shirt fighting with another boy half his size.

"Get your hands off me!" the little boy screamed as the two of them wrestled on the cobblestones. Soon a crowd of children had gathered around, jeering and taunting the fighters.

"Hey, stop fighting!" Robert shouted at them as he pulled the two boys apart. "Go home, all of you."

As the children left one by one, Robert asked, "Who are these children?"

"Ah, pay no mind to them," a local woman answered. "Everyone calls them the white slaves of England. They work twelve hours a day in the mills and sweatshops. Most of their parents are in prison or dead."

Robert's own father had died when he was younger. He could have been one of these poor children. "When do they go to school?" he asked the woman.

"School? They don't go to school. They have to work to live," she answered.

This encounter birthed the seed of an idea in Raike's mind. He was convinced that the church should reach out to these children. Raike started the first Sunday school through his local church. His beginnings were humble. A motley group of destitute boys gathered for lessons every Sunday. The teachers were lay people from the church with no special qualifications.

Other church leaders responded with a mixture of astonishment and criticism. The Bible says nothing, they argued, about meeting the educational needs of the poor—especially on the Sabbath! Despite this opposition, the idea began to catch on. Another Sunday school group started, then another—until the movement had spread all over England and then overseas to the United States. Within a few years, millions of children's lives had been transformed by the Sunday school movement. At one point, almost every child in England and the United States attended Sunday school.

Today, that number has dropped to less than 5 percent in the United Kingdom. Now we need a new church movement—a discipleship movement to reach the world's most vulnerable children. In almost every church, we now see a Sunday school. Why not an Alongsiders group in every church? After all, the call to make disciples is central to the calling of Christians everywhere.

Today, youth and children across the world are becoming disciples of Jesus and going on to disciple others. Lives are changing. Families are changing. The movement is brewing as Alongsiders are slowly but surely building relationships that can change the world. Join the movement, and let us walk alongside those who walk alone.

To donate or partner with Alongsiders International, visit us online: www.alongsiders.org.

NOTES

1. CALLED AND CONFUSED

[1] You can read more about these experiments in my book *Subversive Jesus* (Grand Rapids, MI: Zondervan, 2016), which describes our seven years living in inner-city Vancouver, Canada.

[2] The Downtown Eastside is a tiny, inner-city neighborhood described by the United Nations as "a two-mile stretch of decaying rooming houses, seedy strip bars and shady pawn shops." It is home to more than five thousand addicts; hundreds of women trapped in prostitution; and thousands of homeless people. The Downtown Eastside has been labeled the most concentrated drug and poverty ghetto in North America, with high use of heroin, cocaine, and meth-amphetamine, according to criminologist Benedikt Fischer of Simon Fraser University. It's also the only place in North America where drug addicts can shoot heroin into their veins at an officially sanctioned injection site (Associated Press, "Canada's Olympic City Has Notorious Skid Row," January 30, 2010, NBC News, www.nbcnews.com/id/wbna35160185).

[3] "'Go Ye and Preach the Gospel': Five Do and Die," *Life*, January 30, 1956, 10-19.

[4] This article originally appeared at www.christianitytoday.com/edstetzer/2018 /november/john-chau-missions-and-fools-part-1.html but has now been deleted. It is preserved online: Ed Stetzer, "Ed Stetzer on John Chau, Missionary Work, and Foolishness," Black Christian News, accessed April 14, 2020, https:// blackchristiannews.com/2018/11/ed-stetzer-on-john-chau-missionary-work -and-foolishness/.

[5] This privilege is not only held by white people, of course, especially once you get out of North America. In Asia, for example, missionaries from South Korea, Malaysia, Singapore, and Hong Kong serve in poorer Asian countries with more power and resources than the people who live there. We are all in danger of acting like benevolent gods.

[6]Desmond Tutu, *No Future Without Forgiveness* (New York: Random House, 1999).

2. FROM APOSTLE (INSIDER) TO CATALYST (OUTSIDER)

[1]Ephesians 4 is not an exhaustive list of ministry gifts. Romans 12:4-18 and 1 Corinthians 12:28 also name a number of other gifts and callings. However, because Ephesians 4 has been so widely adopted as a model for church leadership, we will use it as our framework here.

[2]The acronym APEST was popularized by Alan Hirsch to refer to the fivefold ministry described in Ephesians 4. Each of these terms is also found throughout the Bible. For example, *apostle* ("sent one") is used over eighty times in the New Testament. *Prophet* is used nearly 800 times in Scripture and over 150 times in the New Testament. *Evangelist* is also used in Acts and 2 Timothy. *Shepherd* is used twenty-three times in the New Testament. *Teacher* is used 129 times in the New Testament.

[3]The nearest Paul got to a truly foreign culture was in Lystra, where he was in contact with the Lycaonian subculture (Acts 14:11-18).

[4]These points appeared in an earlier form on my blog: Craig Greenfield, "10 Reasons Why Your Good Intentions to Fight Poverty Backfire," *Craig Greenfield* (blog), February 2, 2016, www.craiggreenfield.com/blog/unwisegiving.

[5]I wonder if that deep longing for community that God has placed within every human being explains the popularity of some TV shows, such as *Big Bang Theory*, *Friends*, and *Seinfeld*, which all revolve around a group of friends who share their lives, laughs, and loves at a deep level. We all long for this.

3. DANGER #1: POWER

[1]Material in this section appeared in an earlier form on my blog: Craig Greenfield, "How to Avoid Becoming a 'White Saviour,'" *Craig Greenfield* (blog), October 28, 2016, www.craiggreenfield.com/blog/sidekick.

[2]You can watch the video of Phearom's life and early ministry here: Phearom Nak, *The Story of Phearom*, Alongsiders International, October 20, 2021, video, 3:45, www.youtube.com/watch?v=_TEEM4gP7jI.

[3]Patrisse Cullors and Robert Ross, "The Spiritual Work of Black Lives Matter," *On Being with Krista Tippett*, originally aired February 18, 2016, updated May 25, 2019, The On Being Project, https://onbeing.org/programs/patrisse -cullors-and-robert-ross-the-spiritual-work-of-black-lives-matter-may2017/.

[4]I'm grateful to Rachel Pieh Jones and David Crouch for this insight.

[5]Brian Duignan, "Dunning-Kruger Effect," Encyclopedia Britannica Online, accessed March 7, 2022, www.britannica.com/science/Dunning-Kruger -effect.

[6]This story appeared in an earlier form on my blog: Craig Greenfield, "How to Partner with a Poor Church Without Screwing Everything Up," *Craig Greenfield* (blog), August 18, 2015, www.craiggreenfield.com/blog/2015/8/18 /empowerment.

[7]John L. McKnight and John P. Kretzmann, *Building Communities from the Inside Out: A Path Toward Finding and Mobilizing a Community's Assets* (Chicago: ACTA, 1993).

4. FROM PROPHET (INSIDER) TO ALLY (OUTSIDER)

[1]When H. R. Haldeman's appointment to the White House was announced, Robert Rutland, a close friend and presidential scholar, urged him to start keeping a daily diary recording the major events of each day. Haldeman kept a diary throughout his entire career in the Nixon White House (January 18, 1969–April 30, 1973). The full text of the diaries is almost 750,000 words, and an abridged version was published after Haldeman's death: H. R. Haldeman, *The Haldeman Diaries: Inside the Nixon White House* (New York: G. P. Put-nam's Sons, 1994). A full version is available to researchers at the Richard Nixon Presidential Library and Museum. Quote retrieved from: "Operation Menu," Wikipedia, accessed April 14, 2022, https://en.wikipedia.org/wiki /Operation_Menu.

[2]Ben Kiernan and Taylor Owen, "Roots of U.S. Troubles in Afghanistan: Civilian Bombing Casualties and the Cambodian Precedent," *Asia-Pacific Journal* 8, no. 4 (2010): 6.

[3]Justin Saunders, "U.S. Secret Bombing of Cambodia," *Rabble.ca*, June 9, 2009, https://rabble.ca/toolkit/on-this-day/us-secret-bombing-cambodia.

[4]He later became secretary of state.

[5]Brett S. Morris, "Nixon and the Cambodian Genocide," *Jacobin*, April 27, 2015, www.jacobinmag.com/2015/04/khmer-rouge-cambodian-genocide-united -states.

[6]Ben Kiernan, *How Pol Pot Came to Power: Colonialism, Nationalism, and Communism in Cambodia, 1930–1975*, 2nd ed. (New Haven, CT: Yale University Press, 2004), 13. Quoted in Morris, "Nixon."

[7]Quoted in Morris, "Nixon."

[8]Morris, "Nixon."

[9] According to multiple sources, the US drone program has killed between 9,000 and 17,000 people since 2004. Air Force analyst Daniel Hale says, "With drone warfare, sometimes nine out of 10 people killed are innocent." Josh Marcus, "Air Force Analyst Who Leaked Drone Date Revealing Civilian Deaths Jailed for 45 Months," *Independent*, July 28, 2021, www.independent.co.uk/news/world/americas/daniel-hale-drones-leaked-documents-b1891826.html.

[10] Mech Dara, "Bed Stunt Gets Boeng Kak Women a Year in Jail," *Cambodia Daily*, November 12, 2014, https://english.cambodiadaily.com/news/bed-stunt-gets-boeng-kak-women-a-year-in-jail-72117/.

[11] Much of the material in this section appeared in an earlier form on my blog: Craig Greenfield, "Beyond Thoughts and Prayers—How to Get 'Political' Without Being a Jerk," *Craig Greenfield* (blog), February 17, 2018, www.craiggreenfield.com/blog/2018/2/16/beyond-thoughts-and-prayers-how-to-get-political-without-being-a-jerk; Craig Greenfield, "Yes—Jesus Called Out Corrupt Politicians All the Time," *Craig Greenfield* (blog), January 12, 2021, www.craiggreenfield.com/blog/corruptpoliticians.

[12] Despite its popular association, this quote lacks a proven connection with the writings of Bonhoeffer. See Warren Throckmorton, "The Popular Bonhoeffer Quote That Isn't in Bonhoeffer's Works," *Warren Throckmorton* (blog), August 25, 2016, www.wthrockmorton.com/2016/08/25/the-popular-bonhoeffer-quote-that-isnt-in-bonhoeffers-works/.

[13] Dr. Cornel West, professor of philosophy at Union Theological Seminary and professor emeritus at Princeton University, has said this on more than one occasion. However, it was during his speech at Howard University in April 2011 that West expounded on the phrase and situated it in African American history.

[14] See also Isaiah 20:2-6; Ezekiel 12:3-12, 18-20.

[15] These were not isolated incidents. In fact, here is a partial list of prophetic acts in Scripture: 1 Samuel 15:24-29; 1 Kings 11:29-38; 2 Kings 13:14-19; Nehemiah 5:13; Isaiah 8:1-4; 20:2-6; Jeremiah 7:29; 13:1-11; 16:1-13; 18:1-6; 19:1-13; 25:15-38; 27:1–28:17; 32:6-15, 25, 42-44; 35:1-19; 43:8-13; 51:59-64; Ezekiel 4:1-17; 5:1-17; 12:3-12, 18-20; 21:1-7, 18-22; 24:2-24; 32:17-21; 37:15-23; Hosea 1:2-9; 3:1-5; Micah 1:8; Zechariah 6:9-15; 11:4-17; Luke 10:8-12; Acts 21:8-14; Romans 6:1-7; 1 Corinthians 11:23-26; Revelation 18:21-24.

[16] These words were spoken by Arundhati Roy in her lecture accepting the 2004 Sydney Peace Prize. See Arundhati Roy, "Roy's Full Speech," *Sydney Morning*

Herald, November 4, 2004, www.smh.com.au/national/roys-full-speech
-20041104-gdk1qn.html.

5. DANGER #2: COMPLICITY

[1]Victoria J. Barnett and Barbara Wojhoski, eds., *Dietrich Bonhoeffer Works*, vol. 12, *Berlin: 1932–1933*, ed. Larry L. Rasmussen (Minneapolis: Fortress, 2009), 365.

[2]Contrasting the *developed world* with the *developing world* implies that industrialized nations are somehow better and that other nations should work to be more like them. More neutral terms are *minority world* (to refer to more industrialized nations, which are a minority in terms of the world's population) and *majority world* (to refer to less industrialized nations, which are a majority in terms of the world's population). Many argue that it no longer makes sense to divide the group into just two monolithic groups.

[3]Material from this section on Daniel appeared in an earlier form on my blog: Craig Greenfield, "Of Course It Is Biblical to Repent of Our Nations' Historical Sins," *Craig Greenfield* (blog), June 26, 2021, www.craiggreenfield.com/blog/historicalrepentance.

[4]*Pākehā* is the commonly used word for New Zealand citizens of European origin. Alistair Reese, "Why Pākehā Need to Know Who They Are: Belonging in Aotearoa New Zealand," *Baptist Magazine* (Baptist Churches of New Zealand) 132, no. 1 (2016): 19-21, https://baptistmag.org.nz/why-pakeha-need-to-know-who-they-are/.

[5]Brent Staples, "How Italians Became 'White,'" Opinion, *New York Times*, October 12, 2019, www.nytimes.com/interactive/2019/10/12/opinion/columbus-day-italian-american-racism.html.

[6]Normally, we would limit ourselves to local resources, but we allowed much of the funds for this project to come from overseas because we had decided that the camp would be run from the beginning as a profit-making business. The hope was that this model would be self-sustainable within the country so it would not need ongoing injections to cover operating costs. Such a model is different from a poverty-alleviation project or church plant, both of which need to be primarily resourced from within in order to be replicable. The self-sustaining business model is similar to a microfinance project: the initial loan comes from outside, but the solidarity group is responsible for repaying it, along with a small amount of interest so that another loan can be offered to another group. If well designed, these projects can be financially self-sustainable.

[7] A *tuk-tuk* is a form of simple transportation consisting of a carriage pulled by a small motorbike.

[8] Osheta Moore, *Shalom Sistas: Living Wholeheartedly in a Brokenhearted World* (Harrisonburg, VA: Herald Press, 2017).

[9] Some material in this section appeared in an earlier form on my blog: Craig Greenfield, "Here's the One Essential Biblical Idea to Guide Your Voting," *Craig Greenfield* (blog), October 15, 2020, www.craiggreenfield.com/blog/howtovotelikejesus.

[10] Shane Claiborne, *Executing Grace: How the Death Penalty Killed Jesus and Why It's Killing Us* (San Francisco: HarperOne, 2016).

[11] Origen, *Against Celsus* 5.33.

[12] Brennan Manning, *The Wisdom of Tenderness: What Happens When God's Fierce Mercy Transforms Our Lives* (San Francisco: HarperOne, 2010).

6. FROM EVANGELIST (INSIDER) TO SEEKER (OUTSIDER)

[1] This story appears in an earlier form on by blog: Craig Greenfield, "Isn't It Time for a New Mission Story?," *Craig Greenfield* (blog), November 12, 2019, www.craiggreenfield.com/blog/francischanmissionary.

[2] Staff writer, "Francis Chan Is Moving to Asia Next Year to Be a Missionary," *Christianity Today*, November 8, 2019, www.christiantoday.com/article/francis-chan-is-moving-to-asia-next-year-to-be-a-missionary/133579.htm.

[3] The words of Yin's grandmother's story have been recreated for accuracy from the Khmer Buddhist prophecy recorded here: Athet Pyan Shinthaw Paulu, *Salvation: Your New Relationship with God*, 25-27, http://bibleprobe.com/buddhatoldofjesus.htm.

[4] Ruth A. Tucker, *From Jerusalem to Irian Jaya: A Biographical History of Christian Missions* (Grand Rapids, MI: Zondervan, 1983).

[5] Don Richardson, *Peace Child*, 4th ed. (Minneapolis: Bethany House, 2005).

[6] Richardson, *Peace Child*, 10.

[7] Paulo Freire, *Pedagogy of Freedom: Ethics, Democracy, and Civic Courage*, trans. Patrick Clark (Lanham, MD: Rowman & Littlefield, 1998), 11.

7. DANGER #3: SECULARISM

[1] Maryse Kruithof, "Secularizing Effects of Christian Mission: Fifty Years After Elmer Miller's 'The Christian Missionary, Agent of Secularization,'" *Mission Studies*, published online May 20, 2021, https://brill.com/view/journals/mist/38/1/article-p59_6.xml.

[2]The man who was paralyzed in Acts 3 is in the same position. He is placed outside the temple day after day, but he can only go inside and participate when he experiences God's healing.

8. From Pastor (Insider) to Midwife (Outsider)

[1]The term *shadow pastor* is credited to Curtis Sergeant in Jean Johnson, *We Are Not the Hero: A Missionary's Guide for Sharing Christ, Not a Culture of Dependency* (Sisters, OR: Deep River Books, 2012), chap. 15, Kindle. I have adapted it here to be "shadow leader."

[2]Paulo Freire, *Pedagogy of Freedom: Ethics, Democracy, and Civic Courage*, trans. Patrick Clark (Lanham, MD: Rowman & Littlefield, 1998).

[3]In Ephesians 4:11.

[4]For example, see Exodus 25:6; 30:1, 7-9, 27, 35; 31:8; 35:8, 15, 28; Leviticus 2:1-2, 15-16; 4:7, among others.

[5]As quoted in Daniel Simango, "There Is a Great Need for Contextualisation in Southern Africa," *Studia Historiae Ecclesiasticae* 44, no. 2 (2018), www.scielo.org .za/scielo.php?script=sci_arttext&pid=S1017-04992018000200006.

[6]Jeff Hays, "Religion in Cambodia," *Facts and Details*, https://factsanddetails.com /southeast-asia/Cambodia/sub5_2e/entry-2879.html.

9. Danger #4: Money

[1]These four points appear in an earlier form on my blog: Craig Greenfield, "This Is the Most Common Temptation in Doing Good. Four Reasons You Must Resist," *Craig Greenfield* (blog), March 25, 2017, www.craiggreenfield.com/blog /temptation.

[2]Authoritarian regimes were putting more and more pressure on NGOs, not only in India, but also in Cambodia and beyond.

[3]For example, the Alongsiders movement uses money for printing, developing apps and animations, translation, and gatherings but uses a relatively tiny budget in comparison to its impact across twenty-one countries. Alongsiders mentors and leaders are all volunteers, so the core of the movement is not reliant on funding.

[4]The same problem exists with short-term mission teams that come into communities to do "outreach" that cannot be replicated by local church members. The "disciples" of such efforts learn unattainable forms of outreach.

[5]Jean Johnson, *We Are Not the Hero: A Missionary's Guide for Sharing Christ, Not a Culture of Dependency* (Sisters, OR: Deep River Books, 2012), chap. 9, Kindle.

[6]This observation is by Kenyan evangelist Gideon Kiongo, who is quoted in Johnson, *We Are Not the Hero*, chap. 16, Kindle.

10. From Teacher (Insider) to Guide (Outsider)

[1]This designation was communicated to us by the head of Christian Camping International. Apparently, lots of camps used solar energy or had their own wells for water, but they all drew on the government grid to supplement. We were completely disconnected, simply because connecting to the grid wasn't available to us when we were in the construction phase.

[2]Quoted in Leslie Bentley, "A Brief Biography of Paulo Freire," *Pedagogy and Theatre of the Oppressed*, December 1999, https://ptoweb.org/aboutpto/a-brief -biography-of-paulo-freire/.

[3]OWNED stands for **O**bserve, **W**eep, **N**arrow down, **E**xplore, **D**ecide.

[4]See 1 Corinthians 1:27-31.

11. Danger #5: Individualism

[1]Richard E. Nisbett, *The Geography of Thought: How Asians and Westerners Think Differently . . . and Why* (New York: Free Press, 2003).

[2]Here, I am particularly referring to Westerners descended from Europeans. Others from "Western" countries such as the indigenous Māori people of New Zealand, Asian Americans, Latinos in the United States, etc., may have very different cultural patterns and worldviews.